WHAT IS THE COOPERATIVE PROGRAM?

The Cooperative Program, or CP as some have shortened it, really isn't a program at all. At its core it is a collaborative way of supporting missions both locally and globally. It is a way of combining resources to enable more missions, evangelism and ministry to those in need and those who have yet to hear the gospel. Think of it as a co-op for missions.

Working through the Missions Co-op allows people to pool their resources and talents to:

» feed more hungry people,

» start more churches,

» fund more missionaries,

» reach more people in prisons,

» clothe more needy and

» share the hope of Christ with more people who so desperately need to hear it.

It's more than just financially funding. Through the Missions Co-op, not only are financial gifts combined to do more, but so are mission trips that help us be the hands and feet of Christ while sharing His love. When the 2 million Texas Baptists work together, more people are touched and the duplication of efforts is decreased, enabling more cooperative missions around the state, nation and world. Furthermore, by focusing on key locations, entire areas can be reached through constant relationship building and mission work.

Reaching the world for Christ requires missions cooperation. Be a messenger of Hope.

"But you will receive power when the Holy Spirit comes on you; and you will be my witnesses in Jerusalem, and in all of Judea and Samaria, and to the ends of the earth." **Acts 1:8**

BAPTISTS BUILD HOME FOR FAMILY LIVING IN WATER TANK

LA PRESA GRANDE — On the side of a long dirt road in the middle of nothing special and leading to nothing in particular, the Ramirez family lives behind a thin wire fence. They have little, but they have enough to live. They have few material possessions, but an abundance of joy.

This day – like every Sunday afternoon – the grandparents, who also serve as caretakers, their seven grandchildren and two other families that live close by gather beneath a carport. The young people sing songs and listen to a Bible story before doing crafts and eating a small snack of sugary fruit juice and crackers. A handful of adults circle around a pastor, who shares a weekly Bible lesson.

The movement, vitality and the energy are signs of creation, change and opportunity.

When Mario Garcia, Texas Baptists' River Ministry coordinator in the Laredo area, first came upon the family during a prayer walk excursion, he met grandfather Victorio, who soon introduced his wife Lupe and seven grandchildren, each under the age of 16. Shortly afterward, Garcia discovered that the children lived in one large metal water tank and the grandparents in another.

The containers provided some shelter from the elements, but got as hot as 120 degrees in the summer. When it rained, the tanks leaked. The family had limited electricity and no running water. The family survives on Victorio's pension checks and the grandmother's earnings as a housekeeper, though much of their income helps pay for dialysis to treat Victorio's kidney condition. "That just broke my heart," Garcia said, fighting back the emotion he still feels when he thinks of that moment.

What others might see as a difficult situation Garcia saw as an opportunity to show the character and power of God. He regularly visited the family and built a relationship with them. Finally, he decided to see if he could gather the people and resources needed to build the Ramirez family a new home.

"I think we can show the love of God through our actions," said Garcia, whose ministry is supported by the Mary Hill Davis Offering for Texas Missions. "I have to put it into action. This gives us an open door to show them the love of God through our actions. I can come and read the Bible to them – which is nothing bad, don't get me wrong – I can come and establish a Bible study, but if I know they're living in a water tank, how much better can we show the love of God and His power than building them a house?"

Volunteers, churches and mission groups, particularly Wainwright Baptist Church in Muskogee, Oklahoma, raised the money and did the work for free. They worked quickly and passionately out of a call to help the Ramirez family, Garcia said.

As they worked, they were able to get better acquainted with Victorio and shared the gospel with him. He committed himself to following Christ as did his entire family. Garcia mentioned wanting to start a church in the area, and Victorio volunteered his carport. Now 20-30 people gather there every Sunday afternoon.

"I was overfilled with joy," Victorio said of hearing about the effort to build a house. "It was an opportunity for a big change."

Volunteers recently finished the project and helped the family move their belongings into their new home with ample electricity. The house is wonderful, Garcia said, but it's not nearly as beautiful as the change it's helped bring to the family.

"You can see God's grace, God's power," he said of looking at the house. "One of the goals has been accomplished – for these kids and this family to come to Christ. It's not about the house. That's just been a tool to witness to people and to win them to Christ. And that has given us the opportunity to establish a new church work."

This mission was made possible by a Missions Co-op through Texas Baptists and the Mary Hill Davis Offering for Texas Missions.

WE'RE NO "SUNSHINE" VOLUNTEERS.
WE'RE TEXAS BAPTISTS.

When disaster strikes, here in the U.S. or elsewhere in the world, it's big news. And for days or weeks, it's the focus of headlines, donations, volunteer offers...until the next story comes along. Question is, who sticks around after that first wave of support?

As Christ followers, we can give only one answer: we do. And not just to help in the immediate aftermath of disaster, but throughout the rebuilding process.

Fact is, Texas Baptists have a long history of helping in time of disaster. And whether your contribution comes in the form of prayer, monetary donations or direct volunteer work, it flows to the people who need it in three distinct stages.

STAGE 1 – Respond: the first days and weeks after a disaster.

Texas Baptist Men have been the quick-response team for Texas Baptists for over 40 years. TBM's priority is to share Christ's love through positive reaction and emergency support. They train volunteers and coordinate efforts to provide disaster victims with:

- Emergency food services
- Mobile clean-out and chain saw units
- Temporary emergency child care units
- Shower and laundry units

STAGE 2 – Recover: the weeks and months after a disaster.

After immediate needs are met, and people begin to regain normalcy in their lives, we shift our focus to the church level. Church2Church Partnerships pair up a church within the disaster area with another – usually outside the immediate area – that's willing to assist. Through Community Development, we give practical help during the recovery process. We also provide spiritual support through trained National Organization of Victim Assistance (NOVA) teams and connection to prayer partners.

STAGE 3 – Rebuild: the months and years after a disaster.

Communities often look to the church to play a major role in reestablishing an area. So if the church itself needs repair or rebuilding, that becomes vitally important. Church Building Recovery sends licensed and trained church architects to help church staff and leadership decide:

- What immediate steps are needed to fix the situation?
- What are the best long-term repair or demolition/rebuild options?
- How can new construction best be used for ministry purposes?
- Will the church get sufficient insurance settlements?

To help fund the many aspects of disaster response that Texas Baptists do, please go online and give at texasbaptists.org/give. Or for more information, go to texasbaptists.org/disaster or contact chris.liebrum@texasbaptists.org.

FELLOWSHIP HALL – TAKING A LOOK AT OUR WORLD AGAIN

We pass people each day. And each day we miss seeing their faces, hearing their stories, knowing their need for God.

Often we are focused on the ups and down of our journey, not noticing the people around us and where they are in life – if they too are hurting, celebrating, confused or lonely. We walk down the halls of our own life, our own jobs, our own activities, never opening a door or a window to let others in to join us, to walk with us.

We have good intentions in our lives, and we love Jesus. We may be kind to people, saying a nice "hello, how are you?" when going through the grocery store or coffee shop. But as Christ followers, we aren't called just to be good or nice.

We are called to be something more. We are charged to live out the light, the hope, and the peace that Christ has poured into our lives so that it will overflow to others, pointing them back to Christ. And deep down inside, aren't you ready to be part of something bigger than yourself, to be more than you are right now?

We are called to let the Holy Spirit lead us in the way He wants us to go and to the people He wants us to walk with, being intentional to love them sacrificially and unconditionally as an example of His love.

It's about being part of our community. It's about living life engaged with people who don't know Christ, striving to understand their background and the culture they are in, so that we will know the best way to connect them to the hope of Christ.

This idea of connecting, community and reaching out to those we overlook daily is what the Fellowship Hall is all about. Join the conversation with Texas Baptists as we discuss ways to open our homes, hearts and lives to people we overlook. Through Twitter, Facebook, blogs, YouTube, other social media avenues and a new monthly e-newsletter called Opening Doors, we'll take a look at the faces that pass us each day and see who the Lord leads us to walk beside in His name.

Each month, we will open another door to see how God is working and where He'd like us to join Him in ministering to overlooked people groups in the state. We will explore who the people are, where they live, what life is like for them, ways to get involved and ways to help existing ministries already reaching out to these groups.

This isn't about starting another program or event, but about being a community, a network that is exploring and conversing about what it means to be a Christ follower, seeking to do and say and live out the call God has placed on us to make disciples for Him wherever we are. Let the Fellowship Hall be your portal to taking another look at your world, seeing what mission field is knocking at your doorstep.

FELLOWSHIP HALL
JOIN THE CONVERSATION

Visit www.texasbaptists.org/fellowshiphall to connect with Texas Baptists' social media and to sign up for the monthly Opening Doors e-newsletter.

TEXAS ★ BAPTISTS

BAPTIST GENERAL CONVENTION OF TEXAS
www.texasbaptists.org
333 N. Washington | Dallas, TX 75246-1798 | 888.244.9400

BAPTISTWAY ADULT BIBLE STUDY GUIDE®
LARGE PRINT EDITION

The Corinthian Letters

IMPERATIVES FOR AN IMPERFECT CHURCH

JEFF RAINES
WESLEY SHOTWELL
GARY LONG
CHARLES GLIDEWELL
TOM HOWE

BAPTISTWAYPRESS®
Dallas, Texas

The Corinthian Letters: Imperatives for an Imperfect Church—
BaptistWay Adult Bible Study Guide—Large Print

BAPTISTWAY PRESS® Leadership Team
Associate Executive Director, Baptist General Convention of Texas: Steve Vernon
Director, Education/Discipleship Center: Chris Liebrum
Director, Bible Study/Discipleship Team: Phil Miller
Publisher, BAPTISTWAY PRESS®: Ross West

Cover and Interior Design and Production: Desktop Miracles, Inc.
Printing: Data Reproductions Corporation

First edition: September 2011
ISBN-13: 978-1-934731-76-5

How to Make the Best Use of This Issue

Whether you're the teacher or a student—

1. Start early in the week before your class meets.

2. Overview the study. Review the table of contents and read the study introduction. Try to see how each lesson relates to the overall study.

3. Use your Bible to read and consider prayerfully the Scripture passages for the lesson. (You'll see that each writer has chosen a favorite translation for the lessons in this issue. You're free to use the Bible translation you prefer and compare it with the translation chosen for that unit, of course.)

4. After reading all the Scripture passages in your Bible, then read the writer's comments. The comments are intended to be an aid to your study of the Bible.

5. Read the small articles—"sidebars"—in each lesson. They are intended to provide additional, enrichment information and inspiration and to encourage thought and application.

6. Try to answer for yourself the questions included in each lesson. They're intended to encourage further

thought and application, and they can also be used in the class session itself.

If you're the teacher—

A. Do all of the things just mentioned, of course. As you begin the study with your class, be sure to find a way to help your class know the date on which each lesson will be studied. You might do this in one or more of the following ways:

- In the first session of the study, briefly overview the study by identifying with your class the date on which each lesson will be studied. Lead your class to write the date in the table of contents on page 11 and on the first page of each lesson.

- Make and post a chart that indicates the date on which each lesson will be studied.

- If all of your class has e-mail, send them an e-mail with the dates the lessons will be studied.

- Provide a bookmark with the lesson dates. You may want to include information about your church and then use the bookmark as an outreach tool, too. A model for a bookmark can be downloaded from www.baptistwaypress.org on the Resources for Adults page.

- Develop a sticker with the lesson dates, and place it on the table of contents or on the back cover.

B. Get a copy of the *Teaching Guide*, a companion piece to this *Study Guide*. The *Teaching Guide* contains additional Bible comments plus two teaching plans. The teaching plans in the *Teaching Guide* are intended to provide practical, easy-to-use teaching suggestions that will work in your class.

C. After you've studied the Bible passage, the lesson comments, and other material, use the teaching suggestions in the *Teaching Guide* to help you develop your plan for leading your class in studying each lesson.

D. Teaching resource items for use as handouts are available free at www.baptistwaypress.org.

E. You may want to get the additional adult Bible study comments—*Adult Online Bible Commentary*—by Dr. Jim Denison (president, The Center for Informed Faith, and theologian-in-residence, Baptist General Convention of Texas). Call 1–866–249–1799 or e-mail baptistway@texasbaptists.org to order *Adult Online Bible Commentary*. It is available only in electronic format (PDF) from our website. The price of these comments is $6 for individuals and $25 for a group of five. A church or class that participates in our advance order program for free shipping can receive *Adult Online Bible Commentary* free. Call 1–866–249–1799 or see www.baptistwaypress.org to purchase or for information on participating in our free shipping program for the next study.

F. Additional teaching plans are also available in electronic format (PDF) by calling 1–866–249–1799. The price of these additional teaching plans is $5 for an individual and $20 for a group of five. A church or class that participates in our advance order program for free shipping can receive *Adult Online Teaching Plans* free. Call 1–866–249–1799 or see www.baptistwaypress.org for information on participating in our free shipping program for the next study.

G. You also may want to get the enrichment teaching help that is provided on the internet by the *Baptist Standard* at www.baptiststandard.com. (Other class participants may find this information helpful, too.) Call 214–630–4571 to begin your subscription to the printed or electronic edition of the *Baptist Standard*.

H. Enjoy leading your class in discovering the meaning of the Scripture passages and in applying these passages to their lives.

DO YOU USE A KINDLE?

This BaptistWay *Adult Bible Study Guide* and others are now available in a Kindle edition. The easiest way to find these materials is to search for "BaptistWay" on your Kindle or go to www.amazon.com/kindle and do a search for "BaptistWay." The Kindle edition can be studied not only on a Kindle but also on a PC, Mac, iPhone, Blackberry, or Android phone using the Kindle app available free from amazon.com/kindle.

AUDIO BIBLE STUDY LESSONS

Do you want to use your walk/run/ride, etc. time to study the Bible? Or maybe you're looking for a way to study the Bible when you just can't find time to read? Or maybe you know someone who has difficulty seeing to read even our *Large Print Study Guide*?

Then try our audio Bible study lessons, available on this study plus the *Gospel of Luke, Galatians and 1 & 2 Thessalonians, The Gospel of John: Part One, The Gospel of John: Part Two, Letters of James and John,* and *Profiles in Character.* For more information or to order, call 1–866–249–1799 or e-mail baptistway@texasbaptists.org. The files are downloaded from our website. You'll need an audio player that plays MP3 files (like an iPod®, but many MP3 players are available), or you can listen on a computer.

Writers of This Study Guide

Jeff Raines, writer of lessons one through three, is associate pastor, First Baptist Church, Amarillo, Texas. Dr. Raines is a graduate of Baylor University, Truett Seminary, and Princeton Seminary (D. Min.). He has served as the second vice president of the Baptist General Convention of Texas. He is a frequent writer of Bible study lessons for BaptistWay.

Wesley Shotwell wrote lessons four through six. Dr. Shotwell is pastor of Ash Creek Baptist Church, Azle, Texas. He formerly was pastor of churches in Tennessee. He is a graduate of Baylor University (B.A.), Southwestern Baptist Theological Seminary (M.Div.), and Vanderbilt Divinity School (D.Min.). He is a veteran writer of Bible study lessons for BaptistWay.

Gary Long wrote lessons seven and eight in the *Adult Bible Study Guide* and and also "Teaching Plans" for lessons seven and eight in the *Adult Bible Teaching Guide*. Gary serves First Baptist Church, Gaithersburg, Maryland, as pastor, and formerly served Willow Meadows Baptist Church, Houston, Texas. He has also served churches in North Carolina and Virginia. This is his third set of Bible study curriculum materials for BaptistWay.

Charles Glidewell wrote lessons nine and ten in the *Adult Bible Study Guide* as well as "Teaching Plans" for lessons nine and ten in the *Adult Bible Teaching Guide*. He is the pastor of Cross Roads Baptist Church in Rotan, Texas. He received the Master of Divinity degree from Logsdon Seminary, Abilene, Texas. This is his fourth set of Bible study curriculum materials for BaptistWay.

Tom Howe, who wrote lessons eleven through thirteen, is the senior pastor of Birdville Baptist Church, Haltom City, Texas. Dr. Howe is a graduate of East Texas Baptist University (B.S.), Beeson Divinity School at Samford University (M. Div.), and Southwestern Baptist Theological Seminary (D. Min.). This is his second set of Bible study lessons for BaptistWay.

The Corinthian Letters: Imperatives for an Imperfect Church

DATE OF STUDY

1 CORINTHIANS:

Reports and Questions

Introducing

THE CORINTHIAN LETTERS:
Imperatives for an Imperfect Church

The church at Corinth was imperfect, as all churches are imperfect. In fact, from what we read in 1 and 2 Corinthians, the Christians at Corinth were a troubled church, to say the least. They had issues that divided them and that caused problems among themselves and in their witness to the world. They needed some strong guidance in getting back on the right track. Of course, that could never happen in a church today, could it?

A few years before the Corinthian letters were written, the missionary Paul had come to Corinth proclaiming the good news that people could rise above the despair and debauchery of their first-century world through the power of God. Unlike the gods whom the Corinthians had heard about before, this God had entered directly into human history. In fact, this God had come to live on earth for a brief period of time a few decades before in a man named Jesus.

This Jesus had taught the way of life and given himself sacrificially in death—the worst kind of death, crucifixion as a criminal. Moreover, somehow the meaning of Jesus' death extended to them, making them sense both the depth of their need and the greatness of God's grace. Jesus provided a way to live that meant joy and peace. He called them to follow him in witness and ministry. Even more, this Jesus had been resurrected from the dead! This unbelievable but true event assured them that God would raise followers of Jesus to life after their death, too. The small group had been bonded together by the meaning and hope they had found in Jesus.

Then Paul had gone away. Uncertainty began to develop within the group, and people who had come into the group from various backgrounds began to try to answer the group's questions. Sometimes they tried to say what they thought Paul had really meant when he had said thus and so, and sometimes they tried to offer the religious and philosophical answers they had learned from the surrounding culture. Some of them were pretty adamant in their statements of what they saw as the truth, even questioning, challenging, and rejecting Paul himself.

At the same time, some of the group evidently didn't get very far into the Christian faith. They began to return to the practices and patterns of life they had known in the past. They brought the kind of life they had known on the streets of Corinth into the life of the group. The consensus of at least some of the group was that living in such a manner was no problem now that they had become so spiritual.

Furthermore, bickering, disharmony, divisions, and quarreling began to characterize the group as people claimed to believe first this and then that. They formed cliques and parties based on what they thought they believed various human leaders—Paul, Apollos, Peter— had taught. Some even declared themselves to be above it all. They claimed that they simply followed Christ, looking down their first-century noses at the others.

Finally, someone suggested they should write Paul and ask him about the questions that were being raised. So they did, although the vote was far from unanimous. Perhaps the people who brought the letter to Paul— "Chloe's people"—also brought further news about what was really happening in the congregation (1 Corinthians 1:11).[1]

So Paul wrote the Corinthian Christians. In fact, he wrote several times. The church's problems were so persistent and so great that one letter wouldn't do it. The letters that we have are our 1 and 2 Corinthians, and these letters are the basis for this study.

1 CORINTHIANS: REPORTS AND QUESTIONS

| Lesson 1 | Get Together | 1 Corinthians 1:1–17; 3:1–4 |
| Lesson 2 | Live Morally in an Immoral World | 1 Corinthians 5:1–13 |

NOTES

1. Unless otherwise indicated, all Scripture quotations in "Introducing the Corinthian Letters: Imperatives for an Imperfect Church," "1 Corinthians: Reports and Questions," lessons 7–8, and "2 Corinthians: Renewing the Relationship" are from the New Revised Standard Version Bible.

—1 CORINTHIANS—
Reports and Questions

This study of 1 Corinthians is organized around the reports that had come to Paul about the problems there plus the questions that the Corinthian church asked him directly. From Paul's side of the conversation, we know that reports of divisions (1 Corinthians 1:10), sexual immorality (1 Cor. 5:1), and evidently disbelief in Christ's resurrection (15:12) had come to Paul. Furthermore, we know that the Corinthian Christians asked Paul specific questions about certain issues—marriage (7:1, 25), eating meat that had been sacrificed to idols (8:1), the nature and purpose of spiritual gifts (12:1), and "the collection for the saints" (16:1).[1]

Paul may have had more in mind in writing 1 Corinthians, but at least these items provide an index for the major issues about which Paul wrote in the letter. This study of 1 Corinthians focuses on Paul's response to these reports and questions. Because of the brevity of Paul's treatment of "the collection for the saints" (16:1–4) in 1 Corinthians, this question will be dealt with in the study of 2 Corinthians, since this topic is treated extensively in 2 Corinthians 8—9.

Paul had established the church in Corinth on what we often call his second missionary journey (Acts 18:1–18), probably about A.D. 49. Paul then had spent eighteen months in Corinth, instructing the church. Then he had gone away on further missionary work. When Paul was away, the problems described and dealt with in 1 Corinthians developed.

The letter that we know as 1 Corinthians was at least Paul's second actual letter to the Corinthian church (see 1 Corinthians 5:9), but it is the first letter we have. Likely the time Paul wrote it was the mid–50s A.D.

The Corinthians did not receive Paul's letter with unanimous joy. Rather, many of them questioned and challenged his instructions and Paul himself. The fact that we have 2 Corinthians indicates that the first letter didn't solve the problems the church was having.

As we study 1 Corinthians, we may find ourselves reacting similarly to the Corinthians, questioning and challenging its instructions and Paul himself. The letter deals with some tough subjects and contains "some things," as Peter said of some of Paul's writings, "hard to understand" (2 Peter 3:16).[2] But let us try.

For us, an additional reason 1 Corinthians can be difficult to understand and apply is that the letter provides only one side of the dialogue. We might understand its fine points better if we understood more of the situation to which Paul was writing.

Furthermore, although we must seek ways to appropriately apply Paul's instructions to the church at

Corinth, we do well to beware of coming too readily to a quick application to our lives today. Paul directed his guidance to that church in that setting in that day. As Baptist preacher and professor Dr. Kenneth Chafin wrote about seeking to understand and apply this letter, "What makes this difficult is that Paul intended for everything he said to apply to the Corinthians. He did not label for us that which was related only to local culture and circumstance."[3] That reality calls for humility as we consider how to apply to our lives Paul's guidance to the church at Corinth.

Our task is to seek to understand how Paul's instructions to the Corinthian church apply to us and to do so with the greatest courage we can in looking at our own beliefs and practices. One way of approaching the letter is to ask ourselves how Paul might have stated these instructions for us, particularly the principles behind them. Let us begin.

1 CORINTHIANS: REPORTS AND QUESTIONS

Lesson 1	Get Together	1 Corinthians 1:1–17; 3:1–4
Lesson 2	Live Morally in an Immoral World	1 Corinthians 5:1–13
Lesson 3	Be Christian, Whether Married or Single	1 Corinthians 7:1–17, 25–35
Lesson 4	Wrestle Wisely with Life's Gray Areas	1 Corinthians 8:1–13; 10:23–33
Lesson 5	Use Spiritual Gifts for the Shared Good	1 Corinthians 12:1–14; 12:27—13:3
Lesson 6	Affirm the Resurrection Hope	1 Corinthians 15:3–20, 35–44, 50–57

Additional Resources for Studying 1 Corinthians[4]

Raymond Bryan Brown. "1 Corinthians." *Broadman Bible Commentary*. Volume 10. Nashville, Tennessee: Broadman Press, 1970.

F.F. Bruce. *1 and 2 Corinthians*. New Century Bible. London: Oliphants, 1971.

Kenneth L. Chafin. *1, 2 Corinthians*. The Communicator's Commentary. Waco, Texas: Word Books, Publisher, 1985.

David E. Garland. *1 Corinthians*. Baker Exegetical Commentary on the New Testament. Grand Rapids, Michigan: Baker Academic, 2003.

Fred D. Howard. *1 Corinthians: Guidelines for God's People*. Nashville, Tennessee: Convention Press, 1983.

Craig S. Keener. *1 and 2 Corinthians*. New Cambridge Bible Commentary. New York: Cambridge University Press, 2005.

J.W. MacGorman. *Romans, 1 Corinthians*. The Layman's Bible Book Commentary. Volume 20. Nashville: Broadman Press, 1980.

A.T. Robertson. *Word Pictures in the New Testament*. Volume IV. Nashville, Tennessee: Broadman Press, 1931.

N O T E S

1. A.T. Robertson, *Word Pictures in the New Testament*, vol. IV (Nashville, Tennessee: Broadman Press, 1931), 124, 137, 167, 200. The Corinthians may have inquired also about Apollos (1 Corinthians 16:12).

2. Unless otherwise indicated, all Scripture quotations in "1 Corinthians: Reports and Questions" are from the New Revised Standard Version.

3. Kenneth L. Chafin, *1, 2 Corinthians*, The Communicator's Commentary (Waco, Texas: Word Books, Publisher, 1985), 17.

4. Listing a book does not imply full agreement by the writers or BAPTISTWAY PRESS® with all of its comments.

LESSON ONE
Get Together

MAIN IDEA

Christians' participation in disharmony, divisions, jealousy, and quarreling is incompatible with the cross of Christ and marks them as being spiritually immature.

QUESTION TO EXPLORE

How can we overcome our human tendency to division, disharmony, jealousy, and quarreling?

STUDY AIM

To identify ways to overcome our human tendency to division, disharmony, jealousy, and quarreling, even with fellow Christians

QUICK READ

The first issue Paul addressed in 1 Corinthians was a spirit of disunity. He criticized the Corinthians' boasting and division, and he sought to unify them in Christ.

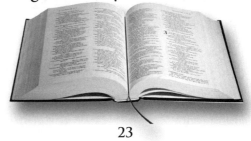

Physics tells us that the universe operates through four fundamental forces: the strong nuclear force, the electromagnetic force, the weak nuclear force, and the gravitational force.[1] When it comes to humankind, I suggest there is an additional, universal force, woven deeply into our sinful natures. This force exerts its relentless power in marriages, families, clubs, friendships, neighborhoods, teams, governments, and workplaces. If gravity draws bodies together, this force drives us apart. We might call it the *dis*unifying force. No one is immune to this force. The workings of this force parody Jesus' promise that "where two or three have gathered together in My name, I am there in their midst" (Matthew 18:20).[2] The *dis*unifying force promises that *where two or more are gathered*, this force will push them apart.

We find disunity just moments after the fall in Genesis 3. When God confronted Adam with his sin, the response revealed the shattering of relationships: "The man said, 'The woman whom *You* gave to be with me, she gave me from the tree, and I ate'" (Genesis 3:12, italics added for emphasis).

When Jesus prayed for us in John 17, he set his sights on this force: "I do not ask on behalf of these alone, but for those also who believe in Me through their word; *that they may all be one*; even as You, Father, are in Me and I in You, that they also may be in Us, so that the world may believe that You sent Me" (John 17:20–21, italics added for emphasis). It would be difficult to find an area where we have let our Lord down so thoroughly.

Church history is filled with disputes, jealousy, discord, and disunity. Denominational groups splinter with regularity (including Baptists). Such disunity has consequences. Paul recognized the destructive power of disunity in the churches within his sphere of influence, and he worked hard in his letters to foster unity and oneness. While we cannot do much about past centuries of Christian division, we can listen attentively to Scripture and strive for unity within our churches.

1 CORINTHIANS 1:1–17

¹ Paul, called as an apostle of Jesus Christ by the will of God, and Sosthenes our brother,

² To the church of God which is at Corinth, to those who have been sanctified in Christ Jesus, saints by calling, with all who in every place call on the name of our Lord Jesus Christ, their Lord and ours:

³ Grace to you and peace from God our Father and the Lord Jesus Christ.

⁴ I thank my God always concerning you for the grace of God which was given you in Christ Jesus,

⁵ that in everything you were enriched in Him, in all speech and all knowledge,

[6] even as the testimony concerning Christ was confirmed in you,

[7] so that you are not lacking in any gift, awaiting eagerly the revelation of our Lord Jesus Christ,

[8] who will also confirm you to the end, blameless in the day of our Lord Jesus Christ.

[9] God is faithful, through whom you were called into fellowship with His Son, Jesus Christ our Lord.

[10] Now I exhort you, brethren, by the name of our Lord Jesus Christ, that you all agree and that there be no divisions among you, but that you be made complete in the same mind and in the same judgment.

[11] For I have been informed concerning you, my brethren, by Chloe's people, that there are quarrels among you.

[12] Now I mean this, that each one of you is saying, "I am of Paul," and "I of Apollos," and "I of Cephas," and "I of Christ."

[13] Has Christ been divided? Paul was not crucified for you, was he? Or were you baptized in the name of Paul?

[14] I thank God that I baptized none of you except Crispus and Gaius,

[15] so that no one would say you were baptized in my name.

[16] Now I did baptize also the household of Stephanas; beyond that, I do not know whether I baptized any other.

[17] For Christ did not send me to baptize, but to preach the gospel, not in cleverness of speech, so that the cross of Christ would not be made void.

1 CORINTHIANS 3:1–4

¹ And I, brethren, could not speak to you as to spiritual men, but as to men of flesh, as to infants in Christ.

² I gave you milk to drink, not solid food; for you were not yet able to receive it. Indeed, even now you are not yet able,

³ for you are still fleshly. For since there is jealousy and strife among you, are you not fleshly, and are you not walking like mere men?

⁴ For when one says, "I am of Paul," and another, "I am of Apollos," are you not mere men?

Prelude (1:1–9)

We may be tempted to rush through the opening verses of Paul's letters, to get past what we may consider the *fluff* of greetings and thanksgivings, to the heart of the issue. For the attentive, however, these introductions speak volumes about Paul, the recipients of the letter, and the message.

Corinth was a unique place. It had been destroyed by the Romans for rebellion in 146 B.C., but it rose again a century later as a Roman colony under the direction of Julius Caesar. Caesar populated it with Roman freedmen—former slaves who often had education and ambition. Its location on the Greek peninsula provided incredible opportunity. North/south traffic through

Greece had to pass through the area, and the dual ports on the east and west made it a major conduit between Rome and the eastern portion of the Empire. Corinth was a melting pot of philosophies and religions, and it was a place where fortune and status were prized. As a wealthy, favored Roman colony, Corinth contrasted sharply with the poorer surrounding countryside of Greece. There was a pride of place to Corinth. Even in these opening verses, Paul worked to remind the Corinthian Christians that they were part of something larger than Corinth and its pagan values.

While Paul addressed many of his letters to the "saints" in the city, he addressed this letter in the first place to the "church" (singular) "at Corinth" (1 Corinthians 1:2). Corinth would have had several house churches, meeting in the homes of some of the wealthier members. This certainly provided fertile soil for disunity or conflict. Christians may have been rallying around their particular house church leader—in essence dividing into teams over against the other house churches. We can also detect evidence of splits within the churches along socio-economic lines (1 Cor. 11:17–22). In using the singular "church," Paul reminded them they were one body together along with "all who in every place call on the name of our Lord Jesus Christ" (1:2). Paul pointed their attention beyond the boundaries of Corinth. They shared a broader unity in Christ with the other churches on the Greek peninsula and with churches around the known world.

Several phrases reminded them of God's grace in their status in Christ. They had neither earned nor bought their position. Instead, they were "saints by calling" (1:2), given grace (1:4), and "enriched in Him" (1:5). Too, they would be *confirmed* "to the end" (1:8), and they were called into "fellowship" (1:9). While their culture valued status, achievement, the buying of influence through extravagant gifts (called benefaction), persuasive rhetoric, and flowery oratory, Paul emphasized the grace of God in their position in Christ. Just as Paul's status as an apostle came from the will of God (1:1), so their status as saints came from God's grace.

Paul's letters typically included a thanksgiving section. In verse 5, Paul thanked God for their "speech and knowledge." These two things proved problematic through the course of the letter. In fact, Paul would sharply criticize their love of oratory, their practice of "spiritual speech" in speaking in tongues (chapters 12—14), and their love of human wisdom and knowledge. Paul could sincerely thank God for their strengths, although such gifts misused can become a curse and a barrier to the Christian "fellowship"[3] mentioned in verse 9.

A Call to Unity (1:10–17)

Paul addressed the heart of the issue for chapters 1—4 in verse 10. Paul exhorted agreement—"the same mind" and "the same judgment." He called on them to set aside *schismata*, the Greek word for *dissension, schism,* or *a tearing apart.*

Paul had received a first-hand report of such divisions from "Chloe's people" (1:11). Evidently the church was dividing up behind leaders, and Paul listed himself, Apollos, Peter, and Christ. While there might have been Christians rallying behind these names, Paul may also have been using these as an absurd example of their behavior. For a letter to be read in the public meeting of the church, perhaps he did not want to name the local leaders who were heading the various parties. Paul may have been tactfully sketching a parody of their behavior under the names of the famous apostles and Christ.[4]

Paul countered this idea by emphasizing that the only one who was crucified and risen as our Lord was Jesus Christ. Paul certainly did not encourage anyone to be a part of a "Paul" party. In the discussion of baptism in verses 14–17, Paul thanked God that not many would be tempted to some idolatrous connection with himself through baptism. The power of the baptizer in the symbolic act is nothing compared to the one behind the symbolism of baptism: Christ.

As we struggle with divisions today, we need to heed Paul's words. Through the amazing growth of communication and media, we have access to preachers, teachers, and thinkers all over the world. These certainly provide incredible new ways to reach out with the gospel. It also provides, however, the possibility of cults of personality around charismatic communicators. We, too, must guard against confusing the messenger and the message.

Interlude (1:18—2:16)

At first glance, this section looks like *rabbit chasing* by Paul as he worked through the ideas of God's wisdom, worldly wisdom, foolishness, his own status, and the work of the Spirit in understanding the gospel. Rather, I believe Paul was still focused on the disunity in Corinth and was subtly undermining the ideas behind it.

Paul started by luring in the Corinthians, describing how unbelieving Jews and Gentiles dismissed the power and wisdom of God in the cross as foolishness. As the Corinthians were saying *amen* with him about those unbelievers, Paul turned to their own background in 1:26. They were *exhibit A* of God taking weakness and foolishness and doing something amazing in salvation.

As they digested what must have seemed an insult, Paul turned to himself in the beginning of chapter 2. There was nothing to boast about in Paul's person, status, or rhetoric. He simply came with the message of the cross.

The chapter ends with the necessity of the Spirit. Again, none of us can boast about our spiritual standing or attainments. All of us are in the category of foolishness transformed by God's power. Paul certainly left no room for boasting in leaders or in rallying behind certain apostles, teachers, or house-church hosts.

Grow Up! (3:1–4)

As chapter 3 begins, Paul's careful subtlety ends. The Corinthians' spirit of division and disunity revealed them to be "infants in Christ." Imagine the icy silence in the room when this part of Paul's letter was first read in their assembly! As 1 Corinthians continues, we can detect arrogance in this church. There was a belief that they were super-spiritual (see 4:6–8) and blessed with the advanced gifts (chapters 12—14). However great their gifts of knowledge and speech were, Paul claimed that the proof of their station in Christ lay in the spirit of their fellowship. We see later in the letter that they could not even celebrate the Lord's Supper in unity (11:17–34).

As a result, Paul's message to them was milk for infants rather than *grown-up* food. While that language might suggest Paul was holding back advanced Christian teaching from them, I do not think that is the case. Secret teaching and advanced teaching were more at home in the pagan religions of Corinth. Paul's message was consistent from his first presentation of the gospel—the foolishness of the cross and God's power in Christ. That they valued presentations of slick and persuasive oratory revealed more about them than it revealed about the message.[5]

Their response to the gospel and their fracturing into cliques classified them as infants.

Such disunity can fester. Around fifty years after this letter, another church leader wrote these words to the Corinthian church:

> We acknowledge that we have been somewhat slow in giving attention to the matters in dispute among you, dear friends, especially the detestable and unholy schism, so alien and strange to those chosen by God, which a few reckless and arrogant persons have kindled to such a pitch of insanity that your good name, once so renowned and loved by all, has been greatly reviled.[6]

I pray that our churches would be free from such discord.

Applying This Lesson to Life

While none of us is immune to jealousy and disunity, we can resist their hold on us, on our relationships, and on our churches. Paul pointed out some steps in these passages.

First, we need to remember that we are saved by grace. This fundamental fact of our faith prevents boasting, arrogance, and pride.

Second, we need to remember that all human leaders and teachers are *human*. Rather than dividing up based on leaders and teachers, we need to carefully evaluate their message or ministry by the gospel and the cross. Jesus is our standard.

Third, we need to seek the mind of Christ. We will never avoid disagreements. As we together seek the mind of Christ, however, we can more closely approach Paul's words in 1 Corinthians 1:10 that we have "the same mind" and "the same judgment."

Fourth, we need to remember the criteria Paul gave for spiritual maturity. Paul would say later in the letter, "If I speak with the tongues of men and of angels, but do not have love, I have become a noisy gong or a clanging cymbal" (13:1). Knowledge and eloquence are fine gifts. The measure Paul gives us, however, is our relationship with others.

WHY HAVE BAPTISTS STRUGGLED WITH UNITY?

Worldwide, more than 1,000 denominational groups have "Baptist" in their name.[7] If God's initial command, "Be fruitful and multiply" (Gen. 1:28), was intended for denominations, we could count ourselves quite faithful! A big part of Baptist history, however, is a failure to live in unity. Historians identify the church formed by John Smyth and Thomas Helwys in Amsterdam in 1609 as the first

Baptist church. Within months of its formation, however, Smyth and Helwys split over baptism.[8] Many other splits and fights have followed.

Why? Some observers have pointed to some core factors of Baptist identity: freedom, a high view of the authority of Scripture, and missions.[9] We cherish freedom, as exemplified by our emphasis on the priesthood of believers, local church autonomy, and religious liberty. Various Baptist expressions of freedom may, from time to time, offend the understanding of Scripture of other Baptists, however. The force holding us together has traditionally been missions. All too often, the pressures of disunity have overcome our common mission as we divide yet again.

EMBRACING UNITY

- Remember that God's grace eliminates any boasting in ourselves or our abilities

- Avoid jealousy by living in gratitude for what God has done for us

- Avoid lining up behind leaders against others

- Remember that Christ is the One we follow in discipleship

- Remember that the nature of our fellowship says volumes about our maturity in Christ

QUESTIONS

1. What have been some of the causes of church disputes you have observed or experienced?

2. What are some ways we can display unity to the world?

3. Do we allow worldly divisions to creep into the church and our fellowship? How do we keep the cross of Christ as the standard rather than any other ideology or philosophy?

4. Is there a unity of rich and poor in your church? How can we foster unity when people are from radically different backgrounds or situations?

N O T E S

1. Richard L. Myers, *The Basics of Physics* (Westport, Connecticut: Greenwood Publishing, 2006), 1.

2. Unless otherwise indicated, all Scripture quotations in lessons 1–3 are from the New American Standard Bible.

3. Baptist New Testament scholar David Garland translates "fellowship" in this case as "common-union" to emphasize the depth of their connection. David Garland, *1 Corinthians* (Grand Rapids, Michigan: Baker Academic, 2003), 35.

4. Garland, 44.

5. Gordon D. Fee, *The First Epistle to the Corinthians* (Grand Rapids, Michigan: William B. Eerdmans, 1987), 125.

6. 1 Clement 1:1 in "The Letter of the Romans to the Corinthians commonly known as First Clement," *The Apostolic Fathers*: Second Edition (Grand Rapids, Michigan: Baker Book House, 1989), 28.

7. See these books by Baptist historian William Brackney: *Baptists in North America: An Historical Perspective* (Malden, Massachusetts: Blackwell Publishing, 2006) and *Historical Dictionary of the Baptists* (Lanham, Maryland: Scarecrow Press, 2009).

8. H. Leon McBeth, *The Baptist Heritage* (Nashville, Tennessee: Broadman Press, 1987), 36–37.

9. Bill J. Leonard, *God's Last and Only Hope: The Fragmentation of the Southern Baptist Convention* (Grand Rapids, Michigan: William B. Eerdmans, 1990), 43.

1 Corinthians 5:1–13

1 Corinthians 5:1–13

LESSON TWO

Live Morally in an Immoral World

MAIN IDEA

A church is to be a community of disciplined moral living in spite of the immoral behavior of the world beyond.

QUESTION TO EXPLORE

How can a church be a community of disciplined moral living without being pharisaical?

STUDY AIM

To summarize Paul's teachings on disciplined moral living in the church and identify practical ways to apply them

QUICK READ

The Corinthian church was ignoring a serious case of sexual immorality. For the sake of their witness in Corinth, Paul urged them to remove the man from their fellowship.

39

Baptists are accustomed to the idea of *walking the aisle* at the end of the service to join or make a public profession of faith. In one Baptist church in Michigan in June 2007, a longtime member walked the aisle in the opposite direction at the *beginning* of the service. She was escorted out in handcuffs by two law enforcement officers after the pastor's 911 call. While the expelled congregant, seventy-one years old, had taught Sunday School at the church for almost fifty years and had regularly tithed her pension income, she had been expelled by the congregation under the leadership of the pastor for "spreading a spirit of cancer and discord."[1]

Although largely neglected in American churches today, the practice of church discipline certainly has warrant in Scripture and a long history in practice. While some form of church discipline is unfortunately necessary, practicing it with grace, appropriateness, confidentiality, and a redemptive spirit is difficult.

In 1 Corinthians 1—4, Paul spoke about the dangers of the divisive spirit of the church in Corinth. Since the church in Corinth would have been a collection of house churches, it is not difficult to imagine rivalries cropping up and leaders jockeying for prominence. Later in the letter we find evidence of disunity along socio-economic lines, with the wealthy neglecting the poorer members of the church (see 1 Corinthians 11:22). Further, the Christians in Corinth were proud and boastful (1 Cor. 4:6, 7, 18). They valued rhetoric, status, and worldly wisdom, and

they would need the reminder that love was more important than speech or knowledge (1 Cor. 13). The last words
of chapter 4 brought quite a threat, however. "What do
you desire? Shall I come to you with a rod, or with love
and a spirit of gentleness?" (4:21).

Why did Paul use such strong language? Chapters 5
and 6 provide the answer. In addition to their problems
with unity, the church in Corinth was destroying its
witness in the community through toleration of a case
of sexual immorality (5:1–13), through public lawsuits
among church members (6:1–8), and through members
visiting prostitutes (6:12–20). In his opening words,
Paul had addressed this letter to "the church of God
which is at Corinth, to those who have been sanctified
in Christ Jesus, saints by calling. . ." (1:2). The issues in
chapters 5 and 6 display a failure to live together under
Christ in a holy way distinct from the pagan world
around them.

1 CORINTHIANS 5:1–13

¹ It is actually reported that there is immorality among
you, and immorality of such a kind as does not exist even
among the Gentiles, that someone has his father's wife.

² You have become arrogant and have not mourned
instead, so that the one who had done this deed would be
removed from your midst.

³ For I, on my part, though absent in body but present in spirit, have already judged him who has so committed this, as though I were present.

⁴ In the name of our Lord Jesus, when you are assembled, and I with you in spirit, with the power of our Lord Jesus,

⁵ I have decided to deliver such a one to Satan for the destruction of his flesh, so that his spirit may be saved in the day of the Lord Jesus.

⁶ Your boasting is not good. Do you not know that a little leaven leavens the whole lump of dough?

⁷ Clean out the old leaven so that you may be a new lump, just as you are in fact unleavened. For Christ our Passover also has been sacrificed.

⁸ Therefore let us celebrate the feast, not with old leaven, nor with the leaven of malice and wickedness, but with the unleavened bread of sincerity and truth.

⁹ I wrote you in my letter not to associate with immoral people;

¹⁰ I did not at all mean with the immoral people of this world, or with the covetous and swindlers, or with idolaters, for then you would have to go out of the world.

¹¹ But actually, I wrote to you not to associate with any so-called brother if he is an immoral person, or covetous, or an idolater, or a reviler, or a drunkard, or a swindler—not even to eat with such a one.

¹² For what have I to do with judging outsiders? Do you not judge those who are within the church?

13 But those who are outside, God judges. REMOVE THE WICKED MAN FROM AMONG YOURSELVES.

A Family Affair (5:1–2)

Later in the letter, Paul responded to issues raised in a correspondence from the Corinthian church (see 7:1). I do not think the issue at hand in chapter 5 was a part of that letter. In all likelihood, some of those traveling between Corinth and Ephesus (1:11; 16:17) reported the scandalous situation to Paul. "Someone has his father's wife" (5:1). This wording suggests that this was not a relationship with the man's biological mother. He was, rather, having an affair with his step-mother. We do not know whether his father was still alive. Paul made a remarkable comment in saying that such a sin "does not exist even among the Gentiles" (5:1).

Prostitution, homosexuality, extramarital affairs, and concubinage were common practices in the first-century Roman world.[2] Corinth stood out particularly in this regard. Several hundred years before Paul wrote, the verb *korinthiazo* came into use: "to act like a Corinthian, i.e., to commit fornication."[3] In the same period, a rumor spread from the rival city of Athens that described 1,000 prostitutes serving at the temple of Aphrodite in Corinth.[4] As a booming city at a major crossroads with two large seaports, Corinth surely fell short as a place of sexual purity and restraint. Paul was appalled, however, that the church in Corinth was sinking *lower* than the culture at large. When it came to sexual morality, the Roman world and the Jewish world shared little in common. Both cultures, however, condemned incest and would have included a relationship with a step-mother under that term.

Paul focused more in this chapter on the church and its need for purity than on the sinner. Instead of confronting this man (the woman was most likely not a part of the church) the church was "arrogant"(5:2). Some scholars interpret this to mean that they were somehow boasting in this man's heinous act. The Corinthian church seemed to revel in their superiority and spiritual advancement in knowledge. Perhaps they were claiming an enlightened toleration with their knowledge lifting them above traditional sexual rules. I think it more likely that Paul was pointing back to their general attitude of spiritual boasting mentioned in chapter 4. Instead of pride in this awful sin, they had a prevailing attitude of boasting. Paul was expressing shock that a church with this kind of sin in its midst could boast about *anything*.

Paul's remedy was removal of this man. Why did the church resist his removal? Drawing on some of the other problems with this group of Christians, this man might have been a wealthy member with high standing in Corinthian society—perhaps even a house church host. In Roman culture, to reject or insult such a patron or supporter would have damaged the reputation of the church and created a powerful new enemy.[5]

Toxic: Handle with Care (5:3–8)

Through the working of the Spirit, Paul regarded himself as present with the Corinthians with the reading of this letter. Together, under the power of Jesus Christ, they would act to remove this man from the church. Paul was asserting remarkable authority, although he regarded this removal as the business of the church. The church was to take the step.[6]

Verse 5 raises numerous questions. How would the church deliver someone to Satan? What would Satan do with or to the man? Was this a death sentence? In removing him from the community of faith, Paul regarded the man as being put into the realm of this world and its ruler, Satan.

Our life context is so different that it is hard to appreciate what removal from the church might mean. When someone is removed from a church today, they can join the church down the street the next week. In Corinth, there was no other Christian church if the house churches acted together.

Paul's primary concern was with purifying the church, but he also kept an eye on the redemption of the sinner. While Satan would not be a willing participant in restoring the man, Paul regarded the man's exile and suffering under Satan as having the potential to destroy the "flesh" element at work in the man's life (5:5). Paul's hope was for the man's ultimate salvation.

Verses 6–8 depict the purity of the church using three metaphors based on first-century practices and Old Testament history. The first metaphor in verse 6 uses the corrupting power of bad leaven in the bread-making process. Unlike yeast, leaven was part of the bread held back from the prior week's dough and worked into the next batch—a sourdough.[7] If bacteria built up, this leaven would corrupt the whole next batch of bread and then the one after that. Each batch would become more toxic. This man's sin had a contagious and toxic effect.

The second metaphor (5:7) shifts to the church as a new batch of dough. The old and toxic were thrown out. They were to become a new batch. Paul quickly added a qualification to this metaphor in the middle of verse 7. With the gospel of grace, Paul often called churches and believers to become what they already were in Christ. Our striving or acting does not earn us our status as saints. That is a gift from God. In the Christian life, we strive to live up to our status in him. Thus, Paul quickly added in verse 7, "just as you are in fact unleavened."

The final image (5:7b–8) describes the church as a perpetual Passover feast. Purity was an essential part of the Jewish Passover celebration. The house was to be swept of leaven and participants consecrated. Such a picture of

purity clashed with the practices of the boastful and morally lax Corinthian church.

Proper Judgments (5:9–13)

The final section of chapter 5 provides the evidence of
Paul's earlier letter to this church. He had written to warn
them about the dangers of allowing unrestrained sin in
their midst. They had misunderstood his advice about
associating with sinners in the same way many Christians
do today. Paul did not call his churches to withdraw from
the world, in a metaphorical *gated community*, away from
sinners. Neither did he call for preaching aimed at the
moral depravity of nonbelievers in our cities or nations.
They were to live, work, and rub elbows right in the midst
of their cities. Paul even told them not to waste their
breath judging the sins of the world. That is God's business. Paul called them to be very concerned, however,
with the nature of their Christian community.

If so-called Christians were living worldly and sinful
lives, then the church should judge them. When Paul
said not to even eat with them, he was speaking to the
bond of table fellowship of first-century meals. Eating
with them implied approval and affirmation in a much
greater way than a casual meal would today. The church
is not to affirm those living in flagrant and rebellious sin.
Paul did not limit this to sins of sexual immorality, for he

also included covetousness, idolatry, bearing false witness, rebelliousness, and thievery. Paul's final phrase in the chapter comes from Deuteronomy 13:5, in a passage emphasizing the importance of the purity and integrity of God's covenant people. For the sake of the church and its witness in the world, removal of the man was necessary.

Implications and Actions

As communities of imperfect "saints," our churches would be very small indeed if we started a process of casting all the sinners out! That was not Paul's intent in this passage. At the same time, the character of our Christian community matters a great deal. When we affirm public sin—whether sins of sexual immorality, greed, or violence—we communicate to our world that we have nothing different to offer in Christ. Jesus provided a model of an appropriate process in Matthew 18:15–18. Start privately, bring in others only as necessary, and have the goal of restoration. Expulsion from the church is a last resort, and in our context one congregation can simply pass on unresolved problems to other congregations.

Restoration is never easy. Those in sin may need to give up cherished leadership or teaching roles. Victims in the church may be deeply opposed to any form of restoration. As difficult as it is, when our churches take seriously our witness and integrity in living disciplined Christian lives, we have the opportunity to show the difference Christ makes.

A COVENANT PEOPLE

In 1 Corinthians 5:1, Paul used the phrase, "immorality of such a kind as does not exist even among the Gentiles." The Greek word for "Gentiles" is *ethnesin*. This is the same word used in the Greek version of the Old Testament (called the Septuagint) for the nations around Israel. In using this word, Paul was describing the Christian congregation in Corinth as God's covenant people—much as Israel was the covenant people in the Old Testament.[8] The quotation in 5:13 reinforced this point. "Remove the wicked man from among yourselves" comes from Deuteronomy 13:5 in a passage about false prophets among Israel.

At several points in the Old Testament, the sin of individuals threatened the community. In Joshua 7, Israel suffered defeat at Ai because of the sin of Achan in keeping some forbidden plunder. Israel could not continue until Achan was removed. The nature of God's covenant people matters as we strive to live up to our status as those "sanctified in Christ Jesus, saints by calling" (1 Cor. 1:2).

CASE STUDY

Imagine opening the local paper one morning to find that a member of the city council has been indicted on charges of corruption and bribery. He also happens to be a prominent and generous member of your church. He serves as a deacon, sings in the choir, and teaches a young adult Bible study class (facts mentioned in the newspaper story). Should the church take action to remove him from any of those positions or to remove him from the church? What would restoration look like?

QUESTIONS

1. How does the idea of judging in 1 Corinthians 5:12–13 fit with Jesus' command, "Do not judge so that you will not be judged" (Matthew 7:1)?

2. If table fellowship was a signal of lifestyle affirmation in Paul's day (1 Cor. 5:11), what would the signals be in your church that someone was in good standing and affirmed?

3. If someone was to be removed from your church, how many people in the congregation should be involved? Should it be just the pastor, the staff, the deacon body, or the whole congregation?

4. What does your church boast about?

N O T E S ───────────────────────

1. Alexandra Alter, "Banned from Church: Reviving an ancient practice, churches are exposing sinners and shunning those who won't repent," *The Wall Street Journal*, January 18, 2008, page W1. http://online.wsj.com/article/SB120061470848399079.html. Accessed 4/7/11.

2. Everett Ferguson, *Backgrounds of Early Christianity*, 2nd ed. (Grand Rapids, Michigan: William B. Eerdmans, 1987), 69.

3. Gordon D. Fee, *The First Epistle to the Corinthians* (Grand Rapids, Michigan: William B. Eerdmans, 1987), 2.

4. Wendell Willis, "Corinth," *Eerdmans' Dictionary of the Bible*, ed. David Noel Freedman (Grand Rapids, Michigan: William B. Eerdmans, 2000).

5. David Garland, *1 Corinthians*, Baker Exegetical Commentary on the New Testament (Baker Academic: Grand Rapids, Michigan, 2003), 163.

6. By translating the beginning of verse 5 with the additional phrase, "I have decided to deliver," the NASB implies too great a role for Paul in removing the man. Paul wanted the church to act to take care of this problem.

7. Garland, 178.

8. Richard Hayes, *First Corinthians* (Louisville, Kentucky: John Knox Press, 1997), 81.

FOCAL TEXT

1 Corinthians
7:1–17, 25–35

BACKGROUND

1 Corinthians 7

LESSON THREE

*Be Christian, Whether
Married or Single*

MAIN IDEA

Whether married or single, Christians are to live in ways that please the Lord.

QUESTION TO EXPLORE

How can both married and single life be lived in ways that please the Lord?

STUDY AIM

To summarize this passage's teachings on marriage and singleness and describe how they apply to our day

QUICK READ

Paul sought to help the church in Corinth understand issues of marriage, widowhood, singleness, and engagement. Walking in devotion to Christ is more important than any particular marital status.

Have you ever sat anxiously listening to a friend or your spouse on an emotionally-charged telephone call? Imagine listening to this half of a conversation: *Oh, wow, is everyone ok? . . . Where are they taking her? . . . Is she in pain? . . . What room? . . . And the baby? . . . Is the doctor there yet? . . . We'll be there as soon as we can!* That conversation can have very different meanings depending on the context. Is it about childbirth or an auto accident? Is the person on the other end of the phone a friend, neighbor, or your own child? We can radically misinterpret meaning when we hear only one side of the conversation.

In many ways, reading New Testament letters can be like listening to half of a phone conversation. This is less of an issue for a book like Romans, where Paul was introducing himself and his theology to a church he had never visited. In that case, Paul spelled out his thinking in great detail. First Corinthians, though, presents some of the greatest challenges of interpretation.

Paul and the Christians in Corinth shared a rich history together. Paul founded the church, spent eighteen months with them, wrote previously, received a letter from them, and received first-hand reports from multiple people. Paul knew the culture of the city, and he knew the church and its leaders. He knew the streets, the smells, the personality conflicts, and the temptations.

Think about when you get together with an old friend. You can name a single person or place, and your friend might burst out laughing. With your shared history and inside jokes, a single word can bring to mind events and experiences an outsider would completely miss. First Corinthians has something of that nature. As a result, we must work hard to understand this letter, and we must be wary of misinterpreting it.

In the first six chapters of the book, Paul has been responding to first-hand reports of problems in the church that compromised the church's witness. In chapter 7, Paul began responding to issues they had raised in a letter. The clue to these issues is the phrase, "now concerning." This phrase will appear in relation to marriage issues (7:1), engagement (7:25), "things sacrificed to idols" (8:1), spiritual gifts (12:1), the offering for the Jerusalem church (16:1), and Apollos's travel plans (16:12 in Greek).

1 CORINTHIANS 7:1–17, 25–35

¹ Now concerning the things about which you wrote, it is good for a man not to touch a woman.

² But because of immoralities, each man is to have his own wife, and each woman is to have her own husband.

³ The husband must fulfill his duty to his wife, and likewise also the wife to her husband.

⁴ The wife does not have authority over her own body, but the husband does; and likewise also the husband does not have authority over his own body, but the wife does.

⁵ Stop depriving one another, except by agreement for a time, so that you may devote yourselves to prayer, and come together again so that Satan will not tempt you because of your lack of self-control.

⁶ But this I say by way of concession, not of command.

⁷ Yet I wish that all men were even as I myself am. However, each man has his own gift from God, one in this manner, and another in that.

⁸ But I say to the unmarried and to widows that it is good for them if they remain even as I.

⁹ But if they do not have self-control, let them marry; for it is better to marry than to burn with passion.

¹⁰ But to the married I give instructions, not I, but the Lord, that the wife should not leave her husband

¹¹ (but if she does leave, she must remain unmarried, or else be reconciled to her husband), and that the husband should not divorce his wife.

¹² But to the rest I say, not the Lord, that if any brother has a wife who is an unbeliever, and she consents to live with him, he must not divorce her.

¹³ And a woman who has an unbelieving husband, and he consents to live with her, she must not send her husband away.

¹⁴ For the unbelieving husband is sanctified through his wife, and the unbelieving wife is sanctified through her believing husband; for otherwise your children are unclean, but now they are holy.

15 Yet if the unbelieving one leaves, let him leave; the brother or the sister is not under bondage in such cases, but God has called us to peace.

16 For how do you know, O wife, whether you will save your husband? Or how do you know, O husband, whether you will save your wife?

17 Only, as the Lord has assigned to each one, as God has called each, in this manner let him walk. And so I direct in all the churches.

•　•

25 Now concerning virgins I have no command of the Lord, but I give an opinion as one who by the mercy of the Lord is trustworthy.

26 I think then that this is good in view of the present distress, that it is good for a man to remain as he is.

27 Are you bound to a wife? Do not seek to be released. Are you released from a wife? Do not seek a wife.

28 But if you marry, you have not sinned; and if a virgin marries, she has not sinned. Yet such will have trouble in this life, and I am trying to spare you.

29 But this I say, brethren, the time has been shortened, so that from now on those who have wives should be as though they had none;

30 and those who weep, as though they did not weep; and those who rejoice, as though they did not rejoice; and those who buy, as though they did not possess;

³¹ and those who use the world, as though they did not make full use of it; for the form of this world is passing away.

³² But I want you to be free from concern. One who is unmarried is concerned about the things of the Lord, how he may please the Lord;

³³ but one who is married is concerned about the things of the world, how he may please his wife,

³⁴ and his interests are divided. The woman who is unmarried, and the virgin, is concerned about the things of the Lord, that she may be holy both in body and spirit; but one who is married is concerned about the things of the world, how she may please her husband.

³⁵ This I say for your own benefit; not to put a restraint upon you, but to promote what is appropriate and to secure undistracted devotion to the Lord.

To Have and to Hold (7:1–9)

The *one-side-of-a-phone call* nature of 1 Corinthians presents great difficulties in interpreting and understanding these opening verses of chapter 7. The Greek manuscripts had no punctuation. Some interpreters have inferred from verse 1 that Paul held an extremely low view of women and of sexuality. They would claim that Paul's advice to the church was "it is good for a man not to touch a woman" (1 Corinthians 7:1b). Marriage, in their interpretation, was a distant second-best for those unable to exercise self-control.

I do not believe that is the proper interpretation given the unfolding of this chapter and Paul's other words about marriage (for example, Ephesians 5:22–33). "It is good for a man not to touch a woman" was likely a quote stating the position of some in Corinth. Some translations put this statement in quotation marks to indicate that it was from their letter to Paul. From what we learn of the church in the first chapters of the book, it would not be out of character if some leaders were claiming sexual abstinence and asceticism (super-spiritual living that shunned anything physical) as a path to advanced spirituality.[1] They may have even pointed to the unmarried Paul as an example as they sought to convince others. What we find in chapter 7, however, is that Paul would primarily advise Christians to remain as they are. Spirituality is not enhanced by marital status whether married, single, widowed, or engaged. In addition, our standing in Christ is not diminished by sexuality when it is expressed in the proper context of marriage.

In verses 2–5, Paul addressed the problem of some spouses withdrawing from sexuality in marriage. This practice may have contributed to the problem of Christians soliciting prostitutes, described in the passage right before this one, in 1 Corinthians 6:15–20. Paul suggested that spouses may together agree to abstain for a special focus on prayer. Such physical abstinence is not a requirement for faithfulness to Christ, however, and taken too far it may instead lead to immorality.

Verse 4 expresses something both commonplace and radical. The idea of a husband having control over his wife's body was assumed in their culture. The equality Paul described of the wife having authority over her husband's body was profoundly new and unexpected. Some interpreters today describe Paul as chauvinistic. They criticize him for not expressing twenty-first century sensibilities about gender equity. Paul, however, took radical steps for the first-century Roman world. In this chapter he consistently spoke to men and women in mutual and equal terms. With this mutual submission, marriage partners were to live faithfully to their covenant vows and faithfully to Christ.

In verse 7, Paul classified celibacy as a gift. As Paul would argue later in the letter (chapters 12—14), spiritual gifts were to be exercised for the good of the church and were not to be badges of spiritual superiority. Paul described the gift of celibacy in a similar way.[2] Paul's celibate life, free of family responsibilities, allowed him to focus all his energy on these young churches. Verses 8–9 apply this logic to those single or widowed. If they had the gift of celibacy, then they should remain single. If not, they should marry.

Until Death Shall Separate Us (7:10–17)

In these verses, Paul moved to the topic of divorce. We need to keep in mind the context of the problems in Corinth expressed in verse 1. Divorces may have been the result of a partner embracing celibacy or even concluding that in Christ their marriage covenant was dissolved. In their culture, divorce was very easy. One partner leaving with the intent of separation was all that was required. There were no legal or governmental processes.[3] Paul began by referencing Jesus' words against divorce (Mark 10:1–12). In verse 12, Paul moved to a topic not mentioned by the Lord—marriages where only one partner was a Christian. Other writings from this period convey the expectations that wives would adopt the religious beliefs and practices of their husbands. Mixed marriages of believers and unbelievers could (and still can) foster a great deal of stress. Paul urged believers in this situation not to initiate divorce.

In verses 14–15, Paul used language of holiness and ritual cleanliness. Some may have been suggesting that continued sexual activity with a pagan spouse would pollute or somehow render the believing spouse unclean. Paul countered in verses 14–15 that the opposite is the case. As one Bible commentator put it, "holiness is . . . contagious."[4] With this language, Paul was not describing a secondhand path to salvation through marriage to a believer. Such relationships provide good opportunities, however, for the unbelieving spouse to, over time, come to faith in Christ.

In many ways, verse 17 provides a summary of Paul's main idea on these matters. The key to the Christian life is not whether one is single or married. Celibacy is a gift and has certain advantages, but it is not for everyone. The key is that we "walk" in Christ, free from immorality and faithful to God.

In verses 17–24, Paul used two more illustrations of this principle. When someone believes, it does not matter whether he is circumcised. Circumcision is no spiritual advantage one way or another. The same applied to slaves in their culture. Paul advised that if freedom was available, then seize it. Neither status, however, gave a spiritual advantage or an occasion for boasting over those in the other situation.

Single-Minded Devotion (7:25–35)

In verse 25, Paul moved to a secondary issue related to marriage and singleness—instruction for those who were engaged. There were probably very few people in the Corinthian house churches who were betrothed, but Paul's instruction reveals both his pastoral concern and the struggles to work out these very practical matters. Paul's guidance follows the same line as the rest of the chapter. Remain as you are. Following through with marriage is good. Too, remaining single is good, and it brings certain practical benefits for ministry and for a special focus on God.

Related to those who marry, Paul warned about "trouble in this life" (1 Cor. 7:28). I do not think he had in mind any stereotypes of *high-maintenance* wives or *couch-potato* husbands. The trouble stems from the nature of our time. In Paul's theology, we live in a unique age—between the initial victory of the resurrection and the final victory of Christ's return. In this time, Christians suffer opposition and persecution, and yet in and through it we are called to live out God's mission for us. Our relationships, our weeping, our rejoicing, our handling of possessions, and our outlook on our work should all be viewed through the filter of Christ's victory and of the destiny of our world. Even marriage is temporary (Luke 20:34–37). Our knowledge of where God is ultimately taking creation should affect how we spend our time and resources, and it should affect our decisions about family and relationships.

Paul returned in 1 Corinthians 7:32–35 to the practical ministry advantage of singleness. Paul lived an itinerate life of travel, hardships, and suffering (see 2 Corinthians 11:21–30). He followed Christ with an abandon that would have been difficult to sustain if he had also been supporting a family. Paul encouraged others who possessed this gift to follow his example.

Implications and Actions

Throughout this chapter Paul dealt with very practical matters faced by the Corinthian church. He wove together topics of marriage, celibacy, singleness, widowhood, divorce, and engagement. In correcting some of the Corinthian practices and teaching, Paul distinguished between some fundamentals and non-fundamentals for Christians.

Clearly, Christians are to avoid "immoralities" (1 Cor. 7:2; the Greek word is *porneia*). We are to honor the wedding covenant and avoid divorce. The Christian life can be fully lived, however, whether married or single. In Corinth, teachers erred by denigrating marriage as somehow beneath full Christians. In some quarters today, the church makes the opposite mistake by viewing singleness as somehow incomplete or inadequate.

Whether married or single, we need to live life in light of the future, investing in what Jesus called, "treasures in heaven" (Matthew 6:19–20). Perhaps Paul provided the best target for all of us, no matter our marital status—". . . undistracted devotion to the Lord" (1 Cor. 7:35).

DIVORCE

Few topics are as painful and (sadly) relevant to our day as divorce. The New Testament mentions divorce just a handful of times. Those passages are: Matthew 5:31–32 and its parallel passage in Luke 16:18; Matthew 19:1–12 and its parallel passage in Mark 10:2–12; and 1 Corinthians 7. Jesus spoke clearly against divorce. In line with his other teaching in the Sermon on the Mount, Jesus exceeded even the rigorous standards of the Pharisees when it came to divorce. As we have seen in this chapter, Paul added an exception to that rule in the case of marriage to an unbeliever.

Our tendency today is to want a list of acceptable exceptions for divorce. Scripture provides no such list. (Perhaps no comprehensive list is possible given the huge variety of cultural circumstances.) Clearly, God desires that we keep our marriage vows. Divorce, whatever the circumstances, brings brokenness. Church families should both foster strong marriages and show compassion to those who have gone through the pain of divorce.

APPLYING THIS LESSON TO LIFE

- For the Christian who is married, covenant vows must be kept, but devotion to God remains the priority.

- For the Christian who is single, freedom from some family responsibilities should be used in ministry and devotion to Jesus.

- Neither status makes one a second-class citizen in God's family. Churches should honor and respect those who follow Paul's example of singleness.

QUESTIONS

1. What are your barriers to "undistracted devotion to the Lord" (7:35)?

2. If you are married, how can your marriage serve the kingdom of God rather than serving as a distraction?

3. How does our mission in this age and our knowledge of Christ's ultimate victory affect your relationships?

4. How do you avoid "immoralities" (7:2) in our immorality-drenched culture?

5. What are the spiritual benefits to being single?

NOTES

1. While such a view clashes with our culture of *anything goes* sexual expression, this was an element of first-century Roman culture. Some philosophical schools promoted celibacy as a superior lifestyle. Some ancient physicians claimed that sexual relations led to poor health. See David E. Garland, *1 Corinthians* (Grand Rapids, Michigan: Baker Academic, 2003), 265.

2. Gordon D. Fee, *The First Epistle to the Corinthians* (Grand Rapids, Michigan: William B. Eerdmans, 1987), 284.

3. Garland, 295.

4. Richard Hayes, *First Corinthians* (Louisville, Kentucky: John Knox Press, 1997), 121.

FOCAL TEXT

1 Corinthians 8:1–13;
10:23–33

BACKGROUND

1 Corinthians 8:1—11:1

LESSON FOUR

Wrestle Wisely with Life's Gray Areas

MAIN IDEA

Even if a practice is not obviously in disobedience to Christian teachings, Christians still may need to refrain from the practice out of loving concern for others and their witness to them.

QUESTION TO EXPLORE

What principles can help in deciding on the best course of action when the Christian choice is not obvious?

STUDY AIM

To identify principles for dealing with areas of life where the Christian choice is not obvious

QUICK READ

Knowledge of Christian freedom must be utilized wisely for the sake of our Christian witness and for our love of others who may not understand our freedom.

Freedom is at the very heart of the gospel. Jesus was abundantly clear when he said, "Then you will know the truth, and the truth will set you free" (John 8:32). Jesus set us free from sin so that we are no longer bound to sin but we are free not to sin. Jesus set us free from the law. No longer do we have to attempt to earn God's approval by slavish obedience to legalistic rituals and religious rites. Acceptance by God is not dependent on whether we eat pork or walk too far on the Sabbath or make a religious pilgrimage. No, we are saved only by the grace of God in Christ. This is something every Christian should know.

The Corinthians had discovered this freedom. Well, at least some of them had. They were free from ritual hand washing and purity laws and dietary regulations. It was the grace of God and only the grace of God that gave them life. They may have been confused or ignorant about much, but they did know Jesus had set them free.[1]

1 CORINTHIANS 8:1–13

[1] Now about food sacrificed to idols: We know that we all possess knowledge. Knowledge puffs up, but love builds up. [2] The man who thinks he knows something does not yet know as he ought to know. [3] But the man who loves God is known by God.

[4] So then, about eating food sacrificed to idols: We know that an idol is nothing at all in the world and that there is no

God but one. [5] For even if there are so-called gods, whether in heaven or on earth (as indeed there are many "gods" and many "lords"), [6] yet for us there is but one God, the Father, from whom all things came and for whom we live; and there is but one Lord, Jesus Christ, through whom all things came and through whom we live.

[7] But not everyone knows this. Some people are still so accustomed to idols that when they eat such food they think of it as having been sacrificed to an idol, and since their conscience is weak, it is defiled. [8] But food does not bring us near to God; we are no worse if we do not eat, and no better if we do.

[9] Be careful, however, that the exercise of your freedom does not become a stumbling block to the weak. [10] For if anyone with a weak conscience sees you who have this knowledge eating in an idol's temple, won't he be emboldened to eat what has been sacrificed to idols? [11] So this weak brother, for whom Christ died, is destroyed by your knowledge. [12] When you sin against your brothers in this way and wound their weak conscience, you sin against Christ. [13] Therefore, if what I eat causes my brother to fall into sin, I will never eat meat again, so that I will not cause him to fall.

1 CORINTHIANS 10:23–33

[23] "Everything is permissible"—but not everything is beneficial. "Everything is permissible"—but not everything

is constructive. [24] Nobody should seek his own good, but the good of others.

[25] Eat anything sold in the meat market without raising questions of conscience, [26] for, "The earth is the Lord's, and everything in it."

[27] If some unbeliever invites you to a meal and you want to go, eat whatever is put before you without raising questions of conscience. [28] But if anyone says to you, "This has been offered in sacrifice," then do not eat it, both for the sake of the man who told you and for conscience' sake — [29] the other man's conscience, I mean, not yours. For why should my freedom be judged by another's conscience? [30] If I take part in the meal with thankfulness, why am I denounced because of something I thank God for?

[31] So whether you eat or drink or whatever you do, do it all for the glory of God. [32] Do not cause anyone to stumble, whether Jews, Greeks or the church of God— [33] even as I try to please everybody in every way. For I am not seeking my own good but the good of many, so that they may be saved.

A Question About Freedom

Evidently a situation had arisen that caused some consternation among the Corinthians. The Corinthians were having a dispute about the limits of their freedom, and so they asked Paul to give them some insight.

Some people in the Corinthian church were uncomfortable with the freedom others enjoyed. They could not get over the memory of their former lives. There were some who once practiced Judaism whose consciences could not dispense with old habits. There were others who were former pagans, and they remembered the sin of their former life in the pagan temples. So, in the church there were some who had joyfully discovered their freedom and some who were still bound by past memories.

In Corinth, there was a pagan temple where people took their best animals to be sacrificed to pagan gods. A small portion of the meat might be burned on the pagan altar, but the rest of the meat was given back to the owner to eat or to be sold in the market. There was no way for the average shopper to tell whether the meat in the market had been used in the pagan temple sacrifices.

Some of the more legalistic Christians in Corinth believed you should not eat meat that had been sacrificed to the pagan gods because by eating it you were participating in idol worship. On the other hand, the Christians who had discovered their freedom in Christ did not mind eating the meat because they thought that the pagan gods did not really exist anyway, and since they did not exist, the meat was being sacrificed to nothing. They saw nothing wrong with eating the meat.

This cavalier attitude offended the more legalistic believers. Furthermore, there might be a new believer who associated eating the meat with idol worship, and the new believer would not understand why a Christian would participate in something with idolatrous undertones. If a mature Christian was eating the meat, did that mean it was acceptable for a Christian to worship idols?

Or, what if you as a liberated Christian were invited to your pagan neighbor's house for a barbeque and they plopped a big T-bone steak on your plate that had, no doubt, been down at the pagan temple that morning? Would your acceptance of that meat be tacit approval of idolatry? Or should believers relish their freedom regardless of the implicit symbolism of supposedly tainted meat?

Wrong or Right?

So, was eating meat sacrificed to idols wrong or right? According to Paul, it depends. Although he quoted what might be a slogan from Gnostic Christians in 1 Corinthians 10:23 (see also 1 Corinthians 6:12), he was quick to acknowledge that simply because something is permissible for a Christian does not mean it is right. Rightness is governed by love more than knowledge (1 Cor. 8:1).

The liberated Christians in Corinth believed they had a moral right to eat the meat. Paul agreed with them. He agreed that since there was only one God the meat was being sacrificed to nothing and therefore it would not hurt anything to eat it. But a deeper principle was at work that was more important than whether a believer had the right to eat the meat.

Mr. King was a man I knew in my first pastorate. Mr. King had been saved sixty years earlier at the age of twenty. He told me about his conversion experience and then boasted, "I haven't played the fiddle since the day I was saved." I could not figure out what becoming a Christian had to do with not playing the fiddle. We even have a fiddle in our church orchestra! Well, we don't have a fiddle; we have a violin. But even so, I could not understand why it was so important to Mr. King that he had not fiddled since becoming a Christian.

I asked someone else about this. I found out Mr. King had played the fiddle in bars and clubs, and he associated fiddle playing with a sinful lifestyle. If he played it again, he would be doing something he associated with his former life.

I wish that in those sixty years he could have come to realize that in Christ he was free, and that there was nothing inherently wrong with playing the fiddle. Nevertheless, his conscience would not allow him to do it. So, was fiddle playing wrong? It was for Mr. King because his conscience associated it with his former life.

In Corinth some of the new believers had come right out of a pagan religion. In their former life, they ate the meat that was sacrificed to idols and associated it with the worship of their pagan gods. They knew that their conversion had turned them away from idol worship and now their consciences would not let them eat this meat. For them, eating the meat was wrong.

Use Freedom for the Benefit of Others

Paul told the Corinthians that even though eating the meat was permissible for Christians, it might not be beneficial for the spiritual well-being of others. Freedom to eat meat was destructive if eating the meat caused a fragile believer to stumble in faith and revert to paganism. Furthermore, a non-Christian might misunderstand Christian freedom and interpret it as hypocrisy, thus destroying the witness of the Christian. In other words, eating the meat might not have anything to do with one's relationship to God, but it might have a lot to do with one's relationship to other people.

A person can be right about something, but there is more for a Christian to consider than just being right. You can have the right doctrine and still be in the wrong. As Paul said in 1 Corinthians 8:1, "Knowledge puffs up, but love builds up." In other words, love trumps knowledge.

Of course, there are some unchristian attitudes that need to be confronted sometimes, and there are times when arguments may arise that are not a matter of conscience but merely a matter of someone's prejudice being irritated. There are situations where someone may be annoyed with your freedom but their faith is not in danger. That is not what Paul was talking about. He was talking about people whose faith may be shattered by our actions. He was talking about unbelievers who may be looking for hypocrisy that damages our witness.

Christian love should not flaunt freedom in front of people whose faith may be endangered by our actions. Whether it be eating meat or playing a fiddle, we should be careful not to destroy the faith of those with a weak conscience, and neither should we use our freedom to damage our witness to unbelievers.

Freedom Not to Do It

We know that we are free in Christ, but love is willing to sacrifice what we know for the sake of building others in faith. Freedom does not mean we are free to do whatever we want. Freedom means we are at liberty to *not* do some things for the sake of others. Love controls freedom.

A preacher of an earlier generation, Dr. H.A. Ironside (1876–1951), told of a church picnic at which a man who had converted to Christianity from Islam was present. According to the illustration, someone offered the man a sandwich. The man asked, "What kind do you have?" The response was that all that was left was ham or pork roast. The man turned down the offer. Knowing the man's background, the person offering the sandwiches continued, "Don't you know that as a Christian you are freed from all those food restrictions and that you can eat pork or ham or anything you want?"

The convert replied, "Yes, I know I am free to eat pork, but I am also free not to eat it. I'm still involved with my family and I know that when I go home once a year, and I come up to my father's door, the first question he will ask me is, 'Have those infidels taught you to eat the filthy hog meat yet?' If I have to say to him, 'Yes, Father,' I will be banished from that home and have no further witness in it. But if I can say, as I have always been able to say, 'No, Father, no pork has ever passed my lips,' then I have admittance to the family circle and I am free to tell them of the joy I have found in Jesus Christ. Therefore, I am free to eat, or I am free not to eat, as the case may be."

Surely that is the kind of thing Paul had in mind when he said, "So whether you eat or drink or whatever you do, do it all for the glory of God. Do not cause anyone to stumble, whether Jews, Greeks, or the church of God. . . . For I am not seeking my own good but the good of many, so that they may be saved" (1 Cor. 10:31–33).

Implications and Actions

I am thankful to know we are free in Christ. We are not bound by legalisms, and neither are we bound to sin anymore. But there is more to consider when making wise decisions of how to live and behave. Decisions of how to use our freedom should be based on love rather than knowledge.

Above all, our freedom should be used to bring glory to God. Flaunting freedom simply because you have the right to do so may not bring glory to God. So be wise.

FACING ISSUES TODAY

Paul did not write to the Corinthians in a vacuum. He was writing in response to information he had heard and to questions they had asked. He had heard from "Chloe's household" (1 Cor. 1:11) about divisions in the church. It had been reported to him (5:1) that there was immorality. The Corinthians had asked questions concerning marriage (7:1), food sacrificed to idols (8:1), proper worship as it related to spiritual gifts (1 Cor. 11—14), and resurrection (1 Cor. 15).

Paul was writing about real issues in a real church at a real time. Think about the issues facing your church. If you could, what issues would you ask Paul about? Do you think the issues that concerned the Corinthians are still relevant in today's church?

QUESTIONS ————————————————————————————

1. Read Romans 14:1—15:6. How do those instructions compare to the instructions Paul gave in 1 Corinthians 8?

2. What issues do Christians face in the twenty-first century that may compare to the issue of eating meat in Corinth?

3. Does Christian freedom really allow us to do whatever we want? What circumstances might cause us to voluntarily limit our freedom?

4. Jesus did not obey the strict Sabbath laws of his day. His actions offended the strict Jews. Was Jesus in conflict with the principles Paul wrote, or are there times when we should live as an example of Christian freedom even if some are offended?

NOTES ————————————————————————

1. Unless otherwise indicated, all Scripture quotations in lessons 4–6, 9–13 are from the New International Version.

LESSON FIVE

*Use Spiritual Gifts
for the Shared Good*

MAIN IDEA

Christians are to use their gifts from God for the shared benefit and unity of the body of Christ.

QUESTION TO EXPLORE

In our individualistic culture, how much does the life Christians share in the body of Christ matter to you?

STUDY AIM

To identify actions I need to take to use my gifts for the shared good and unity of the body of Christ

QUICK READ

The Holy Spirit equips believers with gifts that when used in the context of the church combine with other believers to accomplish God's will.

Many questions have been asked about the Holy Spirit throughout the history of the church. The questioning began at Pentecost when the Spirit came upon the believers and they began to speak in other languages. The people who were there asked one another, "What does this mean?" Others mocked them, thinking they were drunk (Acts 2:12–13).

Questions about the Spirit have divided people ever since. Unfortunately, many in the Baptist tradition have been leery about the work of the Spirit, deathly afraid that if we talk about the Spirit, we will all become charismatic and accidentally raise a hand during a rousing chorus. We certainly do not want to take a chance of getting carried away.

The Corinthians were a divided church. Some seemed to have had an overdose of the Spirit, speaking in tongues and perhaps getting worked into a frenzy during worship. Others in the church must have frowned on such displays. They understood the Spirit to be at work in teaching and preaching and quietly studying the deeper things of the faith. At the very least, they had noticed that people were different when it came to how they functioned in the church. Things have not changed that much, have they?

1 CORINTHIANS 12:1–14, 27–31

¹ Now about spiritual gifts, brothers, I do not want you to be ignorant. ² You know that when you were pagans,

somehow or other you were influenced and led astray to mute idols. ³ Therefore I tell you that no one who is speaking by the Spirit of God says, "Jesus be cursed," and no one can say, "Jesus is Lord," except by the Holy Spirit.

⁴ There are different kinds of gifts, but the same Spirit. ⁵ There are different kinds of service, but the same Lord. ⁶ There are different kinds of working, but the same God works all of them in all men.

⁷ Now to each one the manifestation of the Spirit is given for the common good. ⁸ To one there is given through the Spirit the message of wisdom, to another the message of knowledge by means of the same Spirit, ⁹ to another faith by the same Spirit, to another gifts of healing by that one Spirit, ¹⁰ to another miraculous powers, to another prophecy, to another distinguishing between spirits, to another speaking in different kinds of tongues, and to still another the interpretation of tongues. ¹¹ All these are the work of one and the same Spirit, and he gives them to each one, just as he determines.

¹² The body is a unit, though it is made up of many parts; and though all its parts are many, they form one body. So it is with Christ. ¹³ For we were all baptized by one Spirit into one body—whether Jews or Greeks, slave or free—and we were all given the one Spirit to drink.

¹⁴ Now the body is not made up of one part but of many.

²⁷ Now you are the body of Christ, and each one of you is a part of it. ²⁸ And in the church God has appointed first of all apostles, second prophets, third teachers, then workers of miracles, also those having gifts of healing, those able to help others, those with gifts of administration, and those speaking in different kinds of tongues. ²⁹ Are all apostles? Are all prophets? Are all teachers? Do all work miracles? ³⁰ Do all have gifts of healing? Do all speak in tongues ? Do all interpret? ³¹ But eagerly desire the greater gifts. And now I will show you the most excellent way.

1 CORINTHIANS 13:1–3

¹ If I speak in the tongues of men and of angels, but have not love, I am only a resounding gong or a clanging cymbal. ² If I have the gift of prophecy and can fathom all mysteries and all knowledge, and if I have a faith that can move mountains, but have not love, I am nothing. ³ If I give all I possess to the poor and surrender my body to the flames, but have not love, I gain nothing.

Understanding the Holy Spirit

The Corinthians lacked understanding about how the Spirit was working in them. How could they have unity as a church if the members of the church were so different?

Were there several *spirits* working with different results in different people?

Furthermore, it seems that some of the Corinthians were boasting that they were better Christians (probably the tongue-speakers) because they obviously had more Holy Spirit than others. Boasting like that seldom produces helpful relationships.

The Holy Spirit was sent to unify the church. Unfortunately, the believers in Corinth were divided over the question. Furthermore, the Spirit was supposed to edify the church. In Corinth, however, their misunderstanding was destroying the church.

They decided to ask Paul. Paul responded by shedding some light on the work of the Spirit. First, he reminded them that there was only one Holy Spirit, and that anyone who claimed Jesus as Lord had the Spirit. The same Holy Spirit was working in each person but equipping them in different ways.

Paul introduced them to the concept of spiritual gifts and listed a smattering of the possible gifts the Spirit might give to different individuals in the church. This is not the only place in the New Testament that spiritual gifts are mentioned, and the list is not exhaustive. Other lists are recorded in Romans 12:6–8; Ephesians 4:11; and 1 Peter 4:10–11.

To the Corinthians, Paul listed the gifts of wisdom, knowledge, faith, healing, miraculous powers, prophecy, the distinguishing of spirits, tongues, and the interpretation of tongues. In the latter part of chapter 12, he added to the list apostles, teachers, and administration. Each gift accomplishes something vital in the work of God's kingdom. All of these gifts come from the same Holy Spirit, and yet they manifest themselves in different ways in different people. Every believer has a gift; no believer has all of the gifts.

There is some question about the modern validity of some of the gifts, particularly speaking in tongues. In the context of 1 Corinthians, tongues seems to be referring to unintelligible speech during a moment of spiritual ecstasy, unlike what happened at Pentecost. Some believe speaking in tongues ceased early in the history of the church when it was no longer necessary to validate a person's conversion. Others believe tongues are still a valid gift, although even Paul questioned its usefulness in the context of public worship.

All One Body

The hymn "Onward Christian Soldiers" has a line that reads, "We are not divided, all one body we."[1] The hymn writer must have been reading 1 Corinthians 12.

Paul affirmed that the church is like a body—the body of Christ, in fact. A body has many parts that all work together to make the whole thing work as one. If one part of the body is missing, then it cannot function as intended.

What if you didn't have any fingers? While you would be able to live without fingers, you could not do everything a healthy body is able to do. Or what if you were just one big body part without the other parts? Paul noted that it would be mighty inconvenient if you were one big eyeball without ears or mouth or hands.

Further, the different parts of the body cannot be jealous of the other parts. An ear cannot simply declare itself useless because it does not function as an eye. No, a fully functioning body needs both eyes and ears, not to mention every other part.

The church is like that. Every spiritual gift is like a body part, and the body of Christ does not function properly when missing a part. Therefore, you cannot say people with a gift that is different from yours are not important in your church. Without them, your church would not function properly. Neither can you amputate yourself from the church simply because your gift is not like someone else's.

Occasionally my wife and I go to the symphony. My favorite player is the guy who plays the triangle. He usually does not have a very big part. He sits patiently while everyone else is playing. Then, just at the right moment he stands up and hits the triangle right on cue. It seems like a little thing, but if it were not for that tinkling sound at just the right moment, the symphony would be incomplete. As much as I like the triangle, I am also glad it is not the only instrument in the band. What would it be like if all you had was an orchestra full of triangles? It would be a mess. No, the triangle is only meaningful when it is played in the context of violins and cellos and trumpets and oboes. The composer's will is done only when all contribute their own part.

Sometimes I hear someone say, "I can be just as good a Christian without church." Well, no, you can't. That is like a triangle playing alone. Not only do you need the church to make your part make sense, but the church needs you to do what God designed the church body to do. Without you, the church is incomplete. Without the church, you are nothing more than a tinkling triangle playing alone in a spiritual wilderness. If the body of Christ, the church, is going to accomplish God's will, everyone must function with his or her own spiritual gift.

The Corinthians did not understand that unity is not the same as uniformity. Unity does not mean everyone is the same. Unity means the coming together of diverse elements in order to accomplish a common task that could not be accomplished alone. Uniformity insists that everyone be the same; but it never accomplishes the bigger task.

God's will for the church can be done only with unity, not with uniformity. Unfortunately Christians often resent diversity in the body of Christ, believing that diversity promotes division and strife. In God's plan of giving gifts, however, the opposite is revealed. It is diversity that allows God's will to be done.

A Better Way

The problem with the Corinthians was not that they were not gifted. They had the gifts of the Spirit in their body. The problem with the Corinthians was they did not have love.

Differences become sources of division without love. A lack of love repels people who are different. Paul says that even if you have a gift of speaking in the language of angels, if you do not love, your gift is useless to the church. If you can preach like Peter or be as smart as Paul or have faith like Abraham, but you do not have love, you are less than helpful in the kingdom. Love holds it all together.

No wonder then that the Corinthian church was divided into factions. They did not understand how spiritual gifts worked, that is true. But their main problem was they did not love one another. Love holds the body together.

Love always does what is best for another person without regard to self. Love sees the contributions of another person and rejoices in the gift God has given him or her for the benefit of the church. Love is not jealous of another's gift, and neither does it boast of one's own gift. Love celebrates the diversity of gifts that all work together to form the body of Christ.

Applying This Lesson to Life

Charles Plumb was a U.S. Naval Academy graduate and a fighter pilot in Vietnam. After seventy-five combat missions, his plane was shot down by a surface-to-air missile. Plumb ejected and parachuted into enemy hands. He spent six years in a Communist prison. He survived the ordeal and then began to lecture about lessons learned from that experience.

One day when Plumb and his wife were sitting in a restaurant, a man at another table came up and said, "You're Charles Plumb! You flew jet fighters in Vietnam from the aircraft carrier Kitty Hawk. You were shot down!"

"How in the world do you know that?" Plumb asked.

"I packed your parachute." The man shook his hand and said, "I guess it worked!"

"It sure did. If your chute had not worked, I wouldn't be here today."

Plumb had a hard time sleeping that night thinking about the man. He tried to imagine what the man looked like back then in uniform. "I wondered how many times I might have seen him and not even said 'good morning' or anything else, because you see, I was a fighter pilot, and he was just a mere sailor."

He thought about the many hours the sailor had spent at a long table in the bowels of the ship, unseen by almost everyone, carefully weaving the shrouds and folding the silks of the chute. He had held the fate of someone he did not know in his hands. That lowly sailor was unseen and unsung. What would have happened if he had decided he did not want to do his job anymore? What if he had said to himself, *If I can't be a fighter pilot, I just won't do anything?* But because he did his job, people lived who would have otherwise died.[2]

God has gifted every believer with a spiritual gift for the benefit of the church. Some are fighter pilots while others fold parachutes. All are necessary.

Not all spiritual gifts are as public as others. Not everyone is the preacher, teacher, or leader. Some gifts are practiced unseen and unsung. But even if you are one of the unseen and unsung, if you do what God has gifted you to do in the body of Christ, people will live who would have otherwise died.

TRUTHS ABOUT SPIRITUAL GIFTS

1. One's use of gifts should honor Jesus (1 Cor. 12:3).

2. God is the source of the gifts (12:6).

3. All Christians are gifted (12:7).

4. Gifts are to be used for the common good rather than for personal benefit (12:7).

5. Each gift is necessary for the body's proper functioning (12:14–26).

6. Some gifts are more useful than others in the functioning of the church (12:31; 14:19).

7. Gifts should be used in the spirit of love demonstrated by unselfish concern for the welfare of others (13:1–13).

8. The proper perspective on and use of gifts results in unity, not divisiveness (1 Cor. 12—13.)

CASE STUDY

You have a friend in your Sunday School class who is contemplating dropping out of church. When you talk to her about it she says she feels she does not fit in. She does not feel her presence makes any difference to the church or to the people in the class. What would you say to her? What could your class do to help her fit in better?

QUESTIONS

1. Consider the gifts Paul listed. How does each gift function in your church?

2. Examine yourself. What spiritual gift has God given to you? Check the other lists in the Bible for other suggestions of possible gifts you may possess (Rom. 12:6–8; Eph. 4:11; and 1 Peter 4:10–11). How are you using your gifts in your church?

3. Do you agree or disagree with the statement: "A person cannot be a good Christian without the church." Why do you agree or disagree?

4. Can you think of other spiritual gifts that may not be listed in any of the biblical lists of gifts?

NOTES

1. Words, Sabine Baring-Gould. http://nethymnal.org/htm/o/n/ onwardcs.htm. Accessed 4/20/11.

2. Speaker's Roundtable, *Insights Into Excellence*, 3rd ed. Chapter 16 by Charles Plumb (Executive Books, 1993).

FOCAL TEXT

1 Corinthians 15:3–20,
35–44, 50–57

BACKGROUND

1 Corinthians 15

LESSON SIX

*Affirm the
Resurrection Hope*

MAIN IDEA

The reality of Christ's resurrection assures Christians of their own resurrection.

QUESTION TO EXPLORE

Is this all there is?

STUDY AIM

To explain Paul's teaching on Jesus' resurrection and to testify of my hope of resurrection from the dead

QUICK READ

The resurrection of Jesus reminds us that our faith is not in vain and that when the Lord returns our hopes will be realized by receiving spiritual bodies that are immortal.

After the massive tsunami struck Galle, Sri Lanka, in December 2004, a small Hindu shrine stood partly preserved amid mattress chunks and broken concrete. Parts of the walls remained, as well as several human-size depictions of Hindu gods. Leaning against the broken roof of the shrines was scrawled a hand-lettered sign painted on a scrap of plywood. In the swirling cursive script of the Sinhalese language the sign read, "Is there any hope for refugees like us?"[1]

Most of us are not in the desperate conditions of tsunami-hit Sri Lanka, but we do find ourselves surrounded by death, even in America. Behind our church is a large cemetery in which I have led services for dozens of people. Is there any hope for them? Someday we who still live and breathe will join those who are buried there and in other places like it. Is there any hope for people like us?

1 Corinthians 15:3–20, 35–44, 50–57

³ For what I received I passed on to you as of first importance: that Christ died for our sins according to the Scriptures, ⁴ that he was buried, that he was raised on the third day according to the Scriptures, ⁵ and that he appeared to Peter, and then to the Twelve. ⁶ After that, he appeared to more than five hundred of the brothers at the same time, most of whom are still living, though some have

fallen asleep. ⁷ Then he appeared to James, then to all the apostles, ⁸ and last of all he appeared to me also, as to one abnormally born.

⁹ For I am the least of the apostles and do not even deserve to be called an apostle, because I persecuted the church of God. ¹⁰ But by the grace of God I am what I am, and his grace to me was not without effect. No, I worked harder than all of them—yet not I, but the grace of God that was with me. ¹¹ Whether, then, it was I or they, this is what we preach, and this is what you believed.

¹² But if it is preached that Christ has been raised from the dead, how can some of you say that there is no resurrection of the dead? ¹³ If there is no resurrection of the dead, then not even Christ has been raised. ¹⁴ And if Christ has not been raised, our preaching is useless and so is your faith. ¹⁵ More than that, we are then found to be false witnesses about God, for we have testified about God that he raised Christ from the dead. But he did not raise him if in fact the dead are not raised. ¹⁶ For if the dead are not raised, then Christ has not been raised either. ¹⁷ And if Christ has not been raised, your faith is futile; you are still in your sins. ¹⁸ Then those also who have fallen asleep in Christ are lost. ¹⁹ If only for this life we have hope in Christ, we are to be pitied more than all men.

²⁰ But Christ has indeed been raised from the dead, the firstfruits of those who have fallen asleep.

35 But someone may ask, "How are the dead raised? With what kind of body will they come?" **36** How foolish! What you sow does not come to life unless it dies. **37** When you sow, you do not plant the body that will be, but just a seed, perhaps of wheat or of something else. **38** But God gives it a body as he has determined, and to each kind of seed he gives its own body. **39** All flesh is not the same: Men have one kind of flesh, animals have another, birds another and fish another. **40** There are also heavenly bodies and there are earthly bodies; but the splendor of the heavenly bodies is one kind, and the splendor of the earthly bodies is another. **41** The sun has one kind of splendor, the moon another and the stars another; and star differs from star in splendor.

42 So will it be with the resurrection of the dead. The body that is sown is perishable, it is raised imperishable; **43** it is sown in dishonor, it is raised in glory; it is sown in weakness, it is raised in power; **44** it is sown a natural body, it is raised a spiritual body.

If there is a natural body, there is also a spiritual body.

• •

50 I declare to you, brothers, that flesh and blood cannot inherit the kingdom of God, nor does the perishable inherit the imperishable. **51** Listen, I tell you a mystery: We will not all sleep, but we will all be changed— **52** in a flash, in the twinkling of an eye, at the last trumpet. For the trumpet will sound, the dead will be raised imperishable, and we will be changed. ⁵³ For the perishable must clothe itself with the imperishable, and the mortal with immortality. ⁵⁴ When the perishable has been clothed with the imperishable, and the mortal with immortality, then the saying that is written will come true: "Death has been swallowed up in victory."

⁵⁵ "Where, O death, is your victory?

Where, O death, is your sting?"

⁵⁶ The sting of death is sin, and the power of sin is the law. ⁵⁷ But thanks be to God! He gives us the victory through our Lord Jesus Christ.

We Serve a Risen Savior (15:3–11)

Paul reminded the Corinthians that Christ has been raised from the dead. The resurrection of Jesus is the focal point of the gospel, and our faith hinges on it. If we cannot preach that Christ is raised, there is nothing to preach, and there is no hope.

Paul had passed on the tradition of the gospel when he preached to the Corinthians. He restated the tradition by quoting what may have been an early Christian confession he had learned from other believers. Although it is hard to tell precisely where the quotation ends, it clearly begins in the latter part of verse 3 and probably closes at the end of verse 5. The gospel in a nutshell is that Christ died according to the Scriptures; was buried; and was raised on the third day according to the Scriptures. Not only was he raised, but he also appeared to people after the resurrection, confirming that he is alive. This is the gospel that has been passed down to us just as Paul passed it down to the Corinthians.

One of the reasons Christians believe this is that Jesus appeared to people after he rose from the dead. Who would have believed it had he not appeared to people?

Jesus appeared to poor old Peter, more of a pebble than the solid rock he had sworn to be. But Jesus came to him after he rose and restored him to love and service. To other disciples, Jesus appeared, even to those who had trouble believing like Thomas. Jesus made an appearance to a gathering attended by "more than five hundred" (1 Corinthians 15:6). Jesus also appeared to his brother James. James had had trouble recognizing who Jesus was, but a resurrection appearance, well, that would make anyone reassess the world. Finally, persecutor Paul was convinced when he met the risen Christ on the Damascus road. Paul's belief in the resurrection of Jesus changed him from an apostate to an apostle.

Our Faith Is Not Futile (15:12–20)

Some of the Corinthians were having trouble believing that faith in the risen Christ would result in resurrection for believers. They had been influenced by the Greek philosophy of their culture that denied the possibility of resurrection. They had little trouble believing in the immortality of the soul, but the resurrection of the body was foreign to their way of thinking.

I have some sympathy with the Corinthians who denied the possibility of resurrection. I have performed hundreds of funerals and have yet to have anyone come back to life. The newspaper prints obituaries, but I have never seen resurrection notices. In our experience, belief in resurrection is unreasonable.

But Paul argued just the opposite. Resurrection is not unreasonable because Christ has been raised from the dead. Those who deny the possibility of resurrection have already been proven wrong—unless, that is, they deny that Christ was raised.

If they denied that Christ was raised, then they were denying the whole gospel, for without the resurrection the entire message Paul preached to them was false. If the message was false, then their faith was futile. If their faith was futile, they had no hope and were wasting their lives on a false Savior. If they were worshiping a false Savior, then there was no hope for the future and no hope for the dead, and they were to be pitied for committing their lives to Jesus.

Implied in Paul's argument, however, is that their faith was not futile! The Corinthian Christians knew the message was not false. They had in fact believed it, and it had made a difference in their lives. If their faith was not futile, then the gospel must be true. If the gospel is true, then

Christ has been raised. If Christ has been raised, then resurrection of the dead is a reality!

Christ is raised from the dead. The Corinthians knew it, and we know it too. The resurrection of Christ proved the power of God over the enemy of death and reminds us that even though Jesus was the first to be raised, he won't be the last.

Spiritual Bodies (15:35–44)

What will it be like when the dead are raised? What about people who were lost at sea and their flesh does not exist anymore? Or what about those who are long dead and their bodies are nothing but dust? What about people whose bodies were cremated? How can they experience bodily resurrection?

These questions may seem impossible to answer, but Paul gave us a hint of what resurrection bodies are like. He introduced the concept of spiritual bodies.

Spiritual bodies are different from bodies of flesh. We are familiar with different kinds of bodies in the created world. Paul noted that creatures on earth have different kinds of bodies that distinguish them from one another. Human beings have one kind of body. Animals like birds and fish have other kinds of bodies. We even look at the celestial bodies of the sun, moon, and stars and know that these bodies are different from the bodies of animals. Paul was not a scientist analyzing the chemical make-up of these different bodies. He simply observed that different beings of creation have different kinds of bodies.

In like manner, a spiritual body is a different kind of body. Many theologians speculate a spiritual body will be like Jesus' resurrection body. After the resurrection, Jesus was not confined to space or time.

Paul compared the concept to a seed that is buried in the ground with one kind of body but emerges as a plant with another kind of body. The plant contains the essence of the seed that was planted in the ground, but the plant is different in form and content from the original seed. Our spiritual bodies will be much more than the worn-out bodies that are planted six feet under ground. They will still be us, but they will be much more.

Two caterpillars were on the ground looking up at a butterfly fluttering by over their heads. One caterpillar turned to the other and said, "You couldn't get me up in one of those things in a million years." Well, they just did not know the truth.

The truth is that these old bodies that are confined to space, time, and gravity are going to be changed. We may not be able to imagine it, and it may not seem reasonable, but God can do things we could not imagine in a million years.

We Will All Be Changed (15:50–57)

A spiritual body will be quite a change! A spiritual body will not be subject to the limitations of this world. It will not suffer sickness or death. It will be *clothed with immortality* (15:53).

This change is necessary for living in the next world. Paul said, "Flesh and blood cannot inherit the kingdom of God" (15:50). Just as our physical bodies are appropriate for living in this world, spiritual bodies are appropriate for living in the kingdom of God in the future.

This change will take place when the Lord returns. Some people will be alive when that event occurs, and they will be changed without dying in this world. Those who have died will be resurrected and equipped with spiritual bodies, never to die again.

All of this sounds rather fantastical to many people. It is no wonder the Corinthians were having a hard time believing it. The Corinthian culture, steeped in Greek philosophy, could not rationally grasp what Paul was preaching. Our culture, also steeped in Greek philosophy, has the added barrier of a scientific worldview that calls for experimental data and repeatable phenomena in order to believe something. Resurrection is not a reasonable assumption.

But we do have data to support resurrection. Christ is raised from the dead! Since Christ is raised we know that the power of God is greater than the power of death. No wonder then that Paul could quote Isaiah and Hosea and shout, "'Death has been swallowed up in victory.' 'Where, O death, is your victory? Where, O death, is your sting?'" (15:54–55). Christ is raised and is only the first of many who will follow when he returns to gather us home.

Implications

Not long ago I was driving down I–35 on my way to a conference when I approached the town of Eddy, Texas. My dad is buried in the cemetery there. I decided to stop for a visit. I drove to the back of the cemetery, stopped on the gravel road at the appropriate place, and got out of the car. There I was surrounded by the dead, many of whom are my relatives. On my left were my great-grandmother, who died in the 1930s, and my great-grandfather, who died in the 1950s. To my right lay some cousins, the Keaches, whom I didn't know much about. They had been dead a long time. But before me was my dad's grave. I stood there for a few minutes, staring at the ground, remembering days gone by. But after about five minutes or so I assumed that nothing was going to happen. After all, when you are six feet under, it is pretty certain you have hit a dead end. So I assumed the worst and got back in the car, ready to resume my journey.

I took a different route out of the cemetery and passed by another mourner at another grave. An old man had set up what almost looked like a campsite next to a new grave. He had built a lean-to tent off the side of his station wagon, and he was sitting in a lawn chair under the lean-to, eating a sandwich, watching the grave. I don't know the whole story, but I can imagine that his wife of sixty or seventy years had just died. It looked as if he had been out there for a few days, probably since the funeral. There he sat, right next to her grave, under a lean-to tent, eating a sandwich, watching. I thought, "What is that guy doing? What is he watching for? Doesn't he know that it is a fairly reasonable assumption that nothing is going to happen?"

Then it occurred to me: he believes it. He really believes it. He believes in resurrection hope.

IMMORTALITY AND RESURRECTION

Greek mystery religions, from which many of the Corinthian Christians had been converted, were comfortable with a doctrine of the immortality of the soul. But they had no place for a doctrine for the resurrection of the body. The philosopher Plato espoused dualism, the separation of the body and soul. The soul was immortal, but the body was mortal. At death, the soul might survive, but the body was dead forever.

We are still influenced by a philosophy of dualism. Modern Westerners have a practical theology of the immortality of the soul.

By contrast, the Bible teaches the unity of body and soul. That is why resurrection is vital if we are to have any hope for the future. The resurrection of Christ gives us that hope because it affirms that the whole person has eternal life, not just the soul.

PREACHING TO THE DEAD

A friend occasionally teaches preaching in one of our Texas Baptist universities. As an exercise in preaching, he sometimes takes his preaching class to a cemetery and tells them to preach to the people in their graves. If you were in that class, what would you preach to the dead?[2]

QUESTIONS

1. What are the greatest intellectual barriers you face when it comes to believing in the resurrection of the dead?

2. What can you point to in your life that assures you that your faith is not futile?

3. If Jesus had not been raised from the dead and were still dead, how would your life be different?

4. What is the difference between immortality of the soul and resurrection of the body?

NOTES ——————————————————————————————

1. *Biblical Recorder,* January 13, 2005. See http://www. baptiststandard.com/index.php?option=com_content&task=view &id=3099&Itemid=133. Accessed 4/20/11.

2. Duane Brooks, *This Magnificent Salvation* (Dallas, TX: BaptistWay Press, 2010), 77.

—2 CORINTHIANS—
Renewing the Relationship

The Letter of 2 Corinthians continues Paul's correspondence with likely the most troublesome church he founded. The previous letter, 1 Corinthians, had not solved the church's problems. Rather, 2 Corinthians suggests that the opposition to Paul that can be seen in 1 Corinthians intensified. Some in the Corinthian church questioned, challenged, and even opposed Paul as a Christian leader. The attacks became personal, in fact.

This situation troubled Paul greatly, as it would anyone in his situation. Paul had founded the church at Corinth on his second missionary journey (Acts 18:1–17). He was the church's spiritual father. Rather than respecting his guidance, though, a vocal and influential group within the church opposed him.

Corinth, a seaport in Greece, was a cosmopolitan city. Its morals or lack of them were so well known that *to corinthianize* was a euphemism for sexual debauchery. Thus, although Paul began the church out of the synagogue, many of the Corinthian believers likely were from the rawest of pagan backgrounds. This background is one reason the Corinthian letters reveal the church at Corinth to have been plagued by numerous problems. The problems continued from 1 Corinthians to 2 Corinthians, but the emphasis in 2 Corinthians shifts to a challenge to Paul's leadership and person. Thus, much of 2 Corinthians deals with Paul's defense of his ministry in general and his right to minister to the Corinthian church in particular.

Over and over Paul sought to persuade the Corinthians to return to loyalty to him. Somehow rival teachers were drawing the church away from appreciation of Paul and attention to his instructions, to the detriment of the church. Exactly who these rival teachers were and what they taught, we do not know. What we do know is that they were in the process of convincing the Corinthians that Paul was second-rate as compared to them. Evidently much more was involved than a popularity contest. Rather, Paul was concerned about the direction these rival teachers were leading the Corinthians. Paul believed that the Corinthian church's attraction to these rival leaders was damaging to the church. Thus he used various means to try to remedy the situation so that he and the Corinthians could repair the rift between them.

Unlike other Pauline letters (such as Romans), 2 Corinthians does not contain an extensive theological section followed by an extensive ethical section. Rather, 2 Corinthians begins and ends with a defense by Paul of his apostolic ministry (2 Corinthians 1—7, 10—13). A small middle section encourages participation in the offering for the saints in Jerusalem that Paul was leading in collecting (2 Cor. 8—9).

In some ways, 2 Corinthians is Paul's most personal letter, revealing more of himself and more personal details than any of his other letters. It contains numerous references to Paul's life and to his personal feelings (see, for example, 1:3–10,23–24; 2:1–14; 5:6–11; 6:3–12; 7:2–15; 11:22–29).

Perhaps 2 Corinthians is more like we think a letter to be than most if not all of Paul's other letters are. Too, like some personal letters today, 2 Corinthians tends to jump from topic to topic and back again.

One of the challenges in studying 2 Corinthians in a church Bible study setting is the need to stay within the context of 2 Corinthians as the letter deals with this tug-of-war Paul and opposing church leaders were having and at the same time to find ways to make application to life today. These Bible study lessons attempt to begin with the context in first-century Corinth and to move toward making application in our current context. If we do not begin with the first-century context, we risk imposing our own ideas on Scripture. If we do not seek application to the context of life today, we risk having only a history lesson.

Having only a history lesson is fine in its place, but guiding Bible students in the formation of their lives as Christians is what we must seek as we study and teach. The Scripture passages selected for study are intended to represent the major themes of 2 Corinthians and make application of each of them to life today.[1]

2 CORINTHIANS: RENEWING THE RELATIONSHIP

Lesson 7	Use Your Difficulties to Help Others	2 Corinthians 1:1–11
Lesson 8	Heal Strained Relationships	2 Corinthians 1:12—2:13
Lesson 9	Measure Ministry By the Right Standards	2 Corinthians 2:17—3:6; 4:1–6
Lesson 10	View Life from Eternity	2 Corinthians 4:7—5:10
Lesson 11	Get Motivated to Minister	2 Corinthians 5:11—6:2
Lesson 12	Become Generous in Giving	2 Corinthians 8:1–15; 9:7–8, 11–15
Lesson 13	Rely On God's Grace	2 Corinthians 12:1–10

Additional Resources for Studying 2 Corinthians[2]

Paul Barnett. *The Second Epistle to the Corinthians.* The New International Commentary on the New Testament. Grand Rapids, Michigan: William B. Eerdmans Publishing Company, 1997.

G.R. Beasley-Murray. "2 Corinthians." *The Broadman Bible Commentary.* Volume 11. Nashville, Tennessee: Broadman Press, 1971.

Ernest Best. *Second Corinthians.* Interpretation: A Bible Commentary for Teaching and Preaching. Louisville: John Knox Press, 1987.

F.F. Bruce. *1 and 2 Corinthians*. New Century Bible. London: Oliphants, 1971.

Kenneth L. Chafin. *1, 2 Corinthians*. The Communicator's Commentary. Waco, Texas: Word Books, Publisher, 1985.

David E. Garland. *2 Corinthians*. The New American Commentary. Nashville, Tennessee: Broadman and Holman, 1999.

Brian Harbour. *2 Corinthians: Commissioned to Serve*. Nashville, Tennessee: Convention Press, 1989.

Craig S. Keener. *1 and 2 Corinthians*. New Cambridge Bible Commentary. New York: Cambridge University Press, 2005.

John B. Polhill. *Paul and His Letters*. Nashville, Tennessee: Broadman and Holman Publishers, 1999.

A.T. Robertson. *Word Pictures in the New Testament*. Volume IV. Nashville, Tennessee: Broadman Press, 1931.

J. Paul Sampley. "The Second Letter to the Corinthians." *The New Interpreter's Bible*. Volume XI. Nashville: Abingdon Press, 2000.

NOTES ———————————————

1. Unless otherwise indicated, all Scripture quotations in "2 Corinthians: Renewing the Relationship" and in lessons 7–8 are from the New Revised Standard Version Bible.

2. Listing a book does not imply full agreement by the writers or BAPTISTWAY PRESS® with all of its comments.

LESSON SEVEN

Use Your Difficulties to Help Others

MAIN IDEA

The difficulties of life can become opportunities for receiving God's help and extending it to others.

QUESTION TO EXPLORE

Can God count on us to pass along to others the help God provides in our difficulties?

STUDY AIM

To describe Paul's approach to the difficulties he experienced and analyze how well I am extending God's comfort to others

QUICK READ

To help to heal the relationship between himself and the Corinthians, Paul extended the comfort to them that he himself had known.

As a result of our church's location in the Washington, D.C., area, our church includes members from all over the world, mostly from Africa. These Africans are amazing. Their former lives have been harrowing and danger-filled, clearly far more difficult on average than their counterpart Christians in North America. One man tells how his wife and two of his three children were chopped to death with machetes in a petty tribal war. Some of the stories include disease, especially AIDS. Some wish to return home but cannot because they are political exiles and sure death awaits them on their return. Still others tell of village-wide slaughters and of having to dig mass graves for hundreds of bodies.

These people know about suffering and affliction, and yet they are content. They have painful memories but strong character. They love and serve through the church with deep joy. They live in an abiding sense of peace and are unperturbed by trivial matters in the community of faith. These are people who fully identify with the Apostle Paul in his sufferings alongside his hope that was "unshaken" (2 Corinthians 1:7) They are people who understand that the difficulties of life can become opportunities for receiving God's help and extending it to others.[1]

2 CORINTHIANS 1:1–11

[1] Paul, an apostle of Christ Jesus by the will of God, and Timothy our brother,

To the church of God that is in Corinth, including all the saints throughout Achaia:

2 Grace to you and peace from God our Father and the Lord Jesus Christ.

3 Blessed be the God and Father of our Lord Jesus Christ, the Father of mercies and the God of all consolation, 4 who consoles us in all our affliction, so that we may be able to console those who are in any affliction with the consolation with which we ourselves are consoled by God. 5 For just as the sufferings of Christ are abundant for us, so also our consolation is abundant through Christ. 6 If we are being afflicted, it is for your consolation and salvation; if we are being consoled, it is for your consolation, which you experience when you patiently endure the same sufferings that we are also suffering. 7 Our hope for you is unshaken; for we know that as you share in our sufferings, so also you share in our consolation.

8 We do not want you to be unaware, brothers and sisters, of the affliction we experienced in Asia; for we were so utterly, unbearably crushed that we despaired of life itself. 9 Indeed, we felt that we had received the sentence of death so that we would rely not on ourselves but on God who raises the dead. 10 He who rescued us from so deadly a peril will continue to rescue us; on him we have set our hope that he will rescue us again, 11 as you also join in helping us by your prayers, so that many will give thanks on our behalf for the blessing granted us through the prayers of many.

Greetings (1:1–2)

Paul began 2 Corinthians with his typical greeting. He was co-writing this letter with Timothy, his dear friend and ministry partner. Timothy had worked with the Corinthians before, and so his name was well-known by the original recipients of this letter. Paul reserved the title "apostle" for himself, referring to Timothy as "our brother," hinting at matters of position and authority.

In this greeting Paul also positioned the Corinthian church in relation to all the saints of Achaia, a reminder of the connectedness of Christians everywhere. It is a timely reminder to us modern Christians that we are part of a larger body of believers than just our study group or even our congregation. Indeed, we are called to join from time to time with other congregations in works that are larger than any of us are incapable of doing alone.

We Are Not Alone (1:3–5)

Indeed, we are not alone. God, "the Father of compassion," is "the God of all comfort," and that comfort is available to all believers. We do not suffer alone, Paul informs us, launching into the letter with a blessing. He blessed God and laid out the major framework of the letter, namely that God does not leave us alone in our travail, but actually enters into our suffering with us, offering comfort and consolation.

"Consolation" (NRSV), "comfort" (NIV, NASB), and *encouragement* are all suitable translations. Paul does not seem to be saying that God wants to make us comfortable in our suffering but instead wants us to use that suffering as a passageway to deeper, stronger faith. Instead of focusing on making us *feel better*, God seems to be interested in helping us *grow better*. As Paul was delivered from hardships—yet not exempt from the suffering—God promises to remain with us always.

Bright Hope for Tomorrow (1:6–7)

Paul experienced God's faithfulness in providing him comfort in his suffering. Then Paul extended that comfort to others. The highly relational God who is with us in our suffering wants us to offer bright hope to others.

When we extend comfort to others in their suffering, we should be mindful that this lesson teaches us about how *we ourselves* can learn to approach suffering, not about how *others* ought to. Just because we've *been there, done that, got the t-shirt*, does not mean we know how others feel or how they ought to deal with their pain. Neither can we assume that they are suffering because of some sin, a poor decision, or bad luck. Some people will experience comfort as a result of their suffering, and some will not. The bottom line is that believers who have suffered should be moved toward greater compassion for the suffering of others.

Paul was directly connecting himself and his sufferings to those of the Corinthian community of faith. He saw strength in this connection. Perhaps he was borrowing from the wisdom of Ecclesiastes 4:9–10, "Two are better than one, because they have a good reward for their toil. For it they fall, one will lift up the other; but woe to one who is alone and falls and does not have another to help." Paul was working to make clear that he and the Corinthians were connected through Christ, and that he had greater compassion for them because of the suffering and affliction within his own life.

Crushed but Not Broken (1:8–11)

Paul wanted the Corinthians to know and understand that he had suffered. He continued the motif that when we share in others' sufferings, it brings encouragement. In order to explain this to the Corinthians, he used stark language to describe the peril of his affliction in 1:8: "for we were so utterly, unbearably crushed that we despaired of life itself."

It is not clear what the terrible experience was for Paul. It could have been an attack by wild animals (1 Cor. 15:32). What is clear is that although he may have felt he was about to die, he did not. God rescued him from the deadly peril, giving him the basis for what he would write later, "We are afflicted in every way, but not crushed..." (2 Cor. 4:8). Paul said in that passage, as he did in this lesson's Scripture, that we should clearly understand that God was the source of the power for this remarkable escape from affliction, not Paul's own power.

Feeling as if he had received a death sentence, Paul knew he could not rely on himself, but only on the God of the resurrection. His faith in this God included a trust that God *would continue* to rescue. Paul rested his hope on this firm basis.

Paul's trust in God was active, and he wanted it to be a contagious kind of trust. He included the Corinthians in his story of personal triumph, crediting them for their prayers. It was essential that they understand the role their prayers played, and that as surely as Paul and they shared in afflictions and suffering, they could share in joys and triumphs.

Implications and Actions

Affliction is one price we pay for commitment. Paul encountered many hardships because of his commitment to take the gospel to the Gentiles. Had he chosen to stay in a comfortable place, he could have avoided much pain and suffering. Likewise, we can be sure that our commitment to go wherever God leads will sometimes result in suffering. Such suffering should not deter us from following God, because we know from Paul's experience that these trials will bring growth in us. While these afflictions will draw us closer to God, we should be aware that suffering is part of a package deal.

God rescues and consoles. Paul's testimony to the Corinthians is unmistakable: God rescues. This testimony to the Corinthians is also a good word to us. God continues in the business of rescue and consolation, and we can trust that God will not forsake or forget us in our hour of darkness.

Receiving God's consolation can help us encourage others. Paul perceived one purpose of his suffering was so that he could identify with the Corinthians in their suffering. His logic was that if he understood and experienced suffering and consolation, then he could relate more closely to the Corinthian church from whom he was estranged. Similarly, once we have endured suffering, it better fits us to identify with others who are in pain and to be a source of encouragement to them.

We should both share in the suffering and celebrate the joys. The human tendency is to feel pity when others suffer, and yet we lean toward jealousy when others are successful. In other words, we hardly ever get jealous of someone's suffering, but we are frequently jealous of their joy. We're much more prone to say, "Bless your heart," when someone suffers than to be envious of their affliction. Conversely, we may be more likely to be jealous of good things in others' lives than to celebrate them. Paul believed we should be able to do both. If we share in suffering, we should also share in the joys of God's delivering comfort.

COMFORT, CONSOLATION, AND ENCOURAGEMENT

No less than ten times in these eleven verses, Paul used various forms of a Greek word that means *comfort*, *consolation*, or *encouragement*, depending on the version of the Bible. The word is similar to the word *paraclete* used by Jesus in reference to the Holy Spirit, indicating a kind of advocacy or guidance through adversity.

The heavy emphasis on comfort, consolation, or encouragement leaves no doubt that Paul saw affliction and suffering as an opportunity to identify with the Corinthians and also to come alongside them in suffering.

Paul saw encouragement and comfort as vital roles in the life of the church. What does your church do to encourage and comfort others in times of hardship? How could your church, study group, or Sunday School class use their own difficulties to help others?

QUICK POINTERS FOR EXTENDING GOD'S COMFORT TO OTHERS

- *Not everyone will handle life as you do.* Paul's affliction was unique to him; your suffering is unique to you.

- *Comfort means different things to different people.* Be sensitive to listen to others' needs as they suffer, rather than assuming you already know what they need.

- *Be mindful of life stages as opportunities to provide comfort.* The empty nest, divorce, serious illness, job loss, death, and similar situations provide the opportunity to extend help.

- *Suffering is not always a result of sin.* Adversity in the lives of others is not necessarily a sign of God's judgment.

- *Don't worry about what to do.* Most times your presence in the midst of another's suffering is the biggest thing the person needs. You most likely can't solve the person's problem, but you can stay connected as he or she faces the problem.

BREAKTHROUGHS IN SUFFERING

Suffering sometimes helps break down barriers in life. Sometimes relationships are patched up at a deathbed. Sometimes coming through a serious health difficulty helps a person develop a new perspective on life.

Suffering has a way of readjusting our perspective on what is important in life. What impact has suffering and difficulty had on your life?

QUESTIONS

1. Why did Paul want the Corinthians to know about his sufferings?

2. Do you believe that God causes suffering? allows suffering?

3. What strength or positive change do you think Paul experienced in this passage?

4. Reflect on a time of suffering or affliction that you have personally experienced. How did you grow or change for good as a result?

5. What has been most helpful to you during a time of suffering or affliction?

6. What would you say to a person who "despaired of life itself" (2 Cor. 1:8) and felt as if he or she couldn't go on?

NOTES

1. Unless otherwise indicated, all Scripture quotations in lessons 7–8 are from the New Revised Standard Version Bible.

LESSON EIGHT

Heal Strained Relationships

MAIN IDEA

Healing strained relationships calls for honesty and forthrightness in communication and for a forgiving heart.

QUESTION TO EXPLORE

How is it best to handle strained relationships with others?

STUDY AIM

To identify ways of dealing with strained relationships in my life and how Paul dealt with strained relationships in his

QUICK READ

Paul responded to the strained relationships with the church at Corinth by speaking with sincerity, explaining his position with love, offering forgiveness, and continuing to care.

I learned a hard set of lessons about conflict and strained relationships when I hired a good friend to be the general contractor on a home remodeling project. We weren't very far into the eight-month job when we both realized our friendship might not withstand the project. Tensions grew until one day I absolutely lost it in a rage with some of the subcontractors on the job. I was out of line, and our conversations grew *painful* like Paul's letters in this lesson.

The job was finished, the house was beautiful, and we were within the originally-promised schedule. I eventually apologized for my blow-up, but long after the project was done and we'd stopped speaking. We've made our peace, but the friendship may never be what it could have been without that situation.

Maybe I shouldn't have hired a friend. Or maybe I should have pursued healing in the relationship sooner. Or perhaps if I'd used better methods of conflict resolution, the whole debacle could have been avoided. Either way, I identify with Paul in his pain over the strained relationship with the church at Corinth. Let's study the Scriptures to see how we might avoid the same kind of problems.

2 CORINTHIANS 1:12–24

12 Indeed, this is our boast, the testimony of our conscience: we have behaved in the world with frankness

and godly sincerity, not by earthly wisdom but by the grace of God—and all the more toward you. **13** For we write you nothing other than what you can read and also understand; I hope you will understand until the end— **14** as you have already understood us in part—that on the day of the Lord Jesus we are your boast even as you are our boast.

15 Since I was sure of this, I wanted to come to you first, so that you might have a double favor; **16** I wanted to visit you on my way to Macedonia, and to come back to you from Macedonia and have you send me on to Judea. **17** Was I vacillating when I wanted to do this? Do I make my plans according to ordinary human standards, ready to say "Yes, yes" and "No, no" at the same time? **18** As surely as God is faithful, our word to you has not been "Yes and No." **19** For the Son of God, Jesus Christ, whom we proclaimed among you, Silvanus and Timothy and I, was not "Yes and No"; but in him it is always "Yes." **20** For in him every one of God's promises is a "Yes." For this reason it is through him that we say the "Amen," to the glory of God. **21** But it is God who establishes us with you in Christ and has anointed us, **22** by putting his seal on us and giving us his Spirit in our hearts as a first installment.

23 But I call on God as witness against me: it was to spare you that I did not come again to Corinth. **24** I do not mean to imply that we lord it over your faith; rather, we are workers with you for your joy, because you stand firm in the faith.

2 CORINTHIANS 2:1–13

1 So I made up my mind not to make you another painful visit. **2** For if I cause you pain, who is there to make me glad but the one whom I have pained? **3** And I wrote as I did, so that when I came, I might not suffer pain from those who should have made me rejoice; for I am confident about all of you, that my joy would be the joy of all of you. **4** For I wrote you out of much distress and anguish of heart and with many tears, not to cause you pain, but to let you know the abundant love that I have for you.

5 But if anyone has caused pain, he has caused it not to me, but to some extent—not to exaggerate it—to all of you. **6** This punishment by the majority is enough for such a person; **7** so now instead you should forgive and console him, so that he may not be overwhelmed by excessive sorrow. **8** So I urge you to reaffirm your love for him. **9** I wrote for this reason: to test you and to know whether you are obedient in everything. **10** Anyone whom you forgive, I also forgive. What I have forgiven, if I have forgiven anything, has been for your sake in the presence of Christ. **11** And we do this so that we may not be outwitted by Satan; for we are not ignorant of his designs.

12 When I came to Troas to proclaim the good news of Christ, a door was opened for me in the Lord; **13** but my mind could not rest because I did not find my brother Titus there. So I said farewell to them and went on to Macedonia.

Boasting? (1:12–14)

Paul has a reputation for being boastful and arrogant. To some extent it's true, but in this case we have to examine why Paul was boasting. Paul was confident in his faith, at least as he wrote about it. Sometimes he was overly boastful, but in this instance his boasting was not about himself, but about God and about the Corinthian church.

Paul believed he had acted with godly sincerity, advancing the mission of God through his actions. He'd examined himself and his actions. He felt he had done right by the Corinthian church, and he gave God the credit for all he'd been able to do. Paul boasted in all these things because they were done by God's power and to God's glory. In this case, boasting was good because it pointed to God's greatness, not Paul's.

Those who boast in modern culture are typically pointing to themselves. Athletes brag about their stats, politicians take credit for everything they can to impress their constituents, and even large corporations want us to know what they do for the community, the environment, and education. By contrast, Christians who boast in God are much rarer, and Paul's boasting is a good rejoinder to those who sometimes keep too quiet about God. When Jesus entered Jerusalem in the palm parade (Luke 19:28–40), the Pharisees told Jesus to quiet his disciples who were shouting hosannas and praises for Jesus. Jesus, quoting from the prophet Habakkuk, said, "if they keep quiet, the stones will cry out" (Luke 19:40, NIV; see Habakkuk 2:11).

A Change in Travel Plans (1:15—2:4)

Travel plans can change suddenly in this modern age. Bad weather, flight delays, and equipment failures are all reasons. But Paul used none of these excuses for not returning to Corinth. He had wanted to visit there on his way back to Macedonia, and his failure to do so seemed to have caused some anger among the Corinthians. Paul defended his decision not to travel to Corinth in such a way that we readers are left to believe that the Corinthians considered him undependable because he had broken his promise.

We see Paul vulnerable in this passage. He felt compelled to explain his change in plans, and he went to great lengths to convince the Corinthian Christians to believe him. He compared his faithfulness to God's faithfulness and justified his truthfulness by saying he was sent by God. Therefore, he came and went as God directed, not by any human planning. God's *yes* is dependable, said Paul, and he essentially said it was God who was leading him to change his plans to visit Corinth.

Paul's next step in verse 23 is to call on God as a witness that his reason for choosing to change his plans was because he wanted to spare them pain in his visit. This was a radical move on Paul's part, and it shows the desperate desire in him to convince his listeners that he was truthful. This kind of language really ramps up the tone of things, indicating that Paul was as serious as he could get.

Paul really wanted to avoid "another painful visit," and so instead of making such a visit, Paul sent another painful letter, a letter that is not available to us today. We can't be sure what he wrote, but he said in 2 Corinthians 2:3 that he wrote in such a way so that when he did finally visit, perhaps it would be less painful to be together. His thinking seemed to be that if he cleared the air with a letter, a visit might be better later. However, judging by Paul's defensiveness, it doesn't seem that the Corinthians were happy about the letter. Any future visit was still going to be painful.

To the Corinthians, Paul's change of plans sounded like a *yes* and *no* simultaneously. It was, at minimum, confusing, and it definitely affected the relationship adversely. Paul's statement, "I call on God as witness against me," is strong (2 Cor. 1:23) and shows the seriousness of the matter. Correcting a breach of trust requires serious effort. In Matthew 5:34–37, Jesus taught us that we should make our *yes* a *yes* and our *no* a *no* every time we say it.

One Very Bad Apple (2:5–11)

In this passage, Paul recalled someone who had caused insult or injury to himself on a previous visit. We don't know who the individual was, although some have conjectured wrongly that it was the man who caused offense by sleeping with his father's wife (1 Cor. 5:1–8). We also don't know what this person did to cause such offense, although we are fairly sure it was directed toward Paul.

Whatever the offense, it seems that the *painful letter* referred to by Paul (2 Cor. 2:4) dealt with the issue. The church received the letter and then disciplined the wrongdoer. In verse 6, Paul wrote, "This punishment by the majority is enough for such a person. . . ." Paul positioned himself to offer forgiveness with the possibility of reconciliation. Paul urged that the community deal with this one rotten apple by reaffirming their love for the man (2:8).

Paul aligned himself with the community in his readiness to forgive, indicating that their shared position of grace would undo the designs of Satan. Paul believed that Satan had been at work in the life of the church, and that the act of grace works to undermine the divisiveness of evil. Dealing with sin in a way that leads to reconciliation and forgiveness is a unifier in churches, even today. We gain ground by dealing with our conflict and differences in a more open way.

Restless Nights in Troas (2:12–13)

Paul's counterpart, Titus, had also been in Corinth. Titus was possibly the one who delivered the previously mentioned *painful letter* to Corinth. He would have had instructions from Paul to measure the Corinthians' response and then meet up with him again in Macedonia.

Meanwhile, Paul stopped off in Troas, where a "door was opened." For Paul, that was probably an opportunity to preach the gospel. However, his anxiety had him in such a knot that he hurried along to Macedonia because he couldn't find Titus. The stress of the whole situation was affecting Paul so deeply that he couldn't remain in Troas and preach. He was restless and anxious in Troas. He felt compelled to resolve the matter and to hear a word from Corinth that would alleviate his burden. But there was no relief for Paul, and he remained deeply and properly concerned for them.

This information was significant. Paul, we know from other parts of his writing, was an effective and fervent preacher of the gospel. Sharing the good news of Christ drove him perpetually. It was truly in his spiritual *DNA*. Yet, we see Paul unable to do what he was passionate about, simply because of his worry over the church at Corinth. We might wonder whether Paul did the right thing in leaving the evangelism opportunities in Troas untouched.

We can also see the lost opportunity that needless conflict causes in churches. How many opportunities to reach the lost have our petty conflicts cost us?

Applying This Lesson to Life

Conflict and strain will come to all relationships. In all our spheres of life—home, school, church, or workplace- we need a solid footing to deal with conflict. Paul certainly knew where he stood and what he believed, and that's a good starting point for us, too. If we're going to have healthy conflict and find resolution, we must be clear about what we believe and value. We also need to have flexibility and a willingness to hear what others have to say to us that may be corrective, helpful, or even painful.

Paul's conflict revealed his deep-seated convictions of faith. Do you know yours? Paul's conflict also revealed a deep love for the church and a desire to see things work out for the good.

Reflect on where you stand in relationship to your church. Is it a healthy relationship? How well do you support the mission and direction of your church? Or is there a conflict that's holding you back from contributing your very best to the life of your church?

The time for healing a strained relationship is always *now*. Learn from Paul—don't let the strain of relationships continue to stretch until the relationship is broken.

CONFLICT IN THE CHURCH

Baptists are no strangers to conflict. Our very existence was birthed in conflict between church and state, with early Baptists fighting for their right to religious freedom and practice. Some conflict can be good for the church. But sometimes the effects of conflict and sin can be destructive.

How does your church handle conflict? How do you deal with problem people? Is there a conflict from the past that is holding your church back from being all God wants it to be?

God can use Paul's painful situation with the church at Corinth to help your church deal with conflict. What can you learn from Paul and the Corinthians?

COMMUNICATION TIPS TO HEAL STRAINED RELATIONSHIPS

Paul wrote a painful letter that must have offended the Corinthians, working against his desire to patch things up. Here are some quick pointers on communication to help you avoid the same dilemma:

- Use e-mail only to inform or affirm, never to confront about inflammatory matters.

- Communicate face-to-face. A great portion of our dialog process involves non-verbal cues and body language.

- A gentle tone of voice will allow you to say frank, difficult things.

- Don't mask how you feel. Be open and honest about your feelings and position, but don't be harsh.

- Stay connected. It's easy to cut off emotionally and let the relationship slide further into disrepair. Make the effort, as Paul did, to follow up.

CASE STUDY

Jeff and David work together in a small company. They have never really liked each other. They won't go to lunch together, and they are stiffly cordial at office functions. Sure, they work amicably enough on projects when assigned, but they have a history. David stole Jeff's idea on a project three years ago and took credit for it—at least that's what Jeff says. David says they were collaborating, but even though Jeff never spoke up, Jeff felt unfairly treated when David got more credit than he did.

David wants to patch things up, and he has sent an e-mail of apology. But the apology e-mail stops just short of taking the blame for stealing Jeff's idea. Jeff wonders why he received only a half-hearted apology, and through e-mail, at that.

How would you advise Jeff to respond? How could David have handled this better? How could Jeff have dealt with the problem more effectively sooner?

QUESTIONS

1. Why did Paul boast? When is it appropriate for you to boast?

2. Paul wrote, "For in him every one of God's promises is a 'Yes'" (2 Cor. 1:20). What did he mean? How has this been true in your life?

3. Paul said that he changed his mind about coming to Corinth in order to avoid causing or experiencing more pain in the relationship. When is it a good time to avoid contact with another person or people to avoid more pain?

4. Paul was willing to forgive a person who personally injured him just because the church at Corinth had forgiven him. Can you imagine a scenario where you could forgive another person simply because someone else had forgiven the person? Could you imagine a situation where you would not forgive under such circumstances?

5. Would it have been better for Paul to make the visit to Corinth and endure some emotional pain, or did he do the right thing in sending them the painful letter?

FOCAL TEXT

2 Corinthians
2:17—3:6; 4:1–6

BACKGROUND

2 Corinthians 2:14—4:6

LESSON NINE

*Measure Ministry
By the Right Standards*

MAIN IDEA

Christian ministry should be measured by Christian standards.

QUESTION TO EXPLORE

How should a church's ministry be measured?

STUDY AIM

To identify ways by which Paul evaluated his ministry and to evaluate my ministry and my church's service in light of these standards

QUICK READ

The sincerity of Paul's ministry was something that could be seen by all. The Christians in Corinth were birthed through the proclamation of a simple truth: Jesus Christ is Lord.

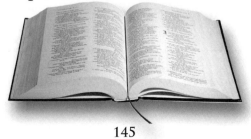

It sometimes seems that for every hard-working, honest minister out there, there are a dozen charlatans (perhaps you can readily name a few). At best these peddlers of the word of God muddy the waters, at worst they lead people astray. It is astonishing that so many false teachers are able to draw the attention and admiration of so many in the church.

This problem is not new. Indeed, the false prophets and wolves began creeping in during the ministries of the first generation of Christians. Pesky peddlers and inflated ministers are not a new phenomenon.

The Apostle Paul sharply distinguished himself from the false teachers in his day. Although Paul's adversaries sought to discredit him and his ministry in the eyes of the Corinthians, he did not lose heart. For Paul the guide for judging any ministry was quite clear: Christian ministry should be measured by Christian standards.[1]

2 CORINTHIANS 2:17

For we are not peddlers of God's word like so many; but in Christ we speak as persons of sincerity, as persons sent from God and standing in his presence.

2 CORINTHIANS 3:1–6

[1] Are we beginning to commend ourselves again? Surely we do not need, as some do, letters of recommendation

to you or from you, do we? [2] You yourselves are our letter, written on our hearts, to be known and read by all; [3] and you show that you are a letter of Christ, prepared by us, written not with ink but with the Spirit of the living God, not on tablets of stone but on tablets of human hearts.

[4] Such is the confidence that we have through Christ toward God. [5] Not that we are competent of ourselves to claim anything as coming from us; our competence is from God, [6] who has made us competent to be ministers of a new covenant, not of letter but of spirit; for the letter kills, but the Spirit gives life.

2 CORINTHIANS 4:1–6

[1] Therefore, since it is by God's mercy that we are engaged in this ministry, we do not lose heart. [2] We have renounced the shameful things that one hides; we refuse to practice cunning or to falsify God's word; but by the open statement of the truth we commend ourselves to the conscience of everyone in the sight of God. [3] And even if our gospel is veiled, it is veiled to those who are perishing. [4] In their case the god of this world has blinded the minds of the unbelievers, to keep them from seeing the light of the gospel of the glory of Christ, who is the image of God. [5] For we do not proclaim ourselves; we proclaim Jesus Christ as Lord and ourselves as your slaves for Jesus' sake. [6] For it is the God who said, "Let light shine out of

darkness," who has shone in our hearts to give the light of the knowledge of the glory of God in the face of Jesus Christ.

People of Sincerity, Sent from God (2:17—3:6)

Based on what Paul wrote in 2 Corinthians, we can reconstruct a portrait of his opponents. Consider three general observations: First, these teachers were known for really selling themselves, talking themselves up, even bringing "letters of recommendation" (2 Corinthians 3:1)[2] in order to gain support for themselves and their views (2 Cor. 3:1; 4:5). Second, Paul's opponents were Jews who were teaching and advocating the old covenant (3:3, 6–9). Finally, these teachers were eloquent speakers, and they doubted Paul's authority because he apparently was not (10:10; 11:5–6).

From the beginning of our focal text, Paul made one thing perfectly clear. He and his partners in ministry were not peddlers of the word of God, but rather people who faithfully served as ministers of a new covenant. Throughout our focal text for this lesson, Paul identified the following measurements of ministry: acting with sincerity as people sent from God (2:17); seeking to help people be more like Christ (3:1–3); relying on God for competence (3:5); focusing on the life-giving nature of the new covenant (3:6); being open, honest, and above-board

(4:1–2); proclaiming "Jesus Christ as Lord" (4:5); being servants of others for Jesus' sake (4:5).

Verses 2 and 3 contain two key concepts that sum up the measurements of Paul's ministry listed in the previous paragraph. The first is Paul's love and true concern for the people at Corinth. Verse 2 says that the Corinthians themselves were Paul's letter of commendation and not only that, but a letter written on the hearts of Paul and his companions. Paul alluded to his care for the Corinthians again in verse 3. According to the New International Version, verse 3 reads, "You show that you are a letter from Christ, *the result of our ministry. . .*" (italics added for emphasis). The New American Standard Bible makes the same point, but gives a more literal translation of the Greek. It reads, "being manifested that you are a letter of Christ, *cared for by us. . .*" (italics added for emphasis). Comparing these translations enables us to be sure to capture the fullness of what Paul was saying. Paul's ministry in Corinth was not just any ministry. The Corinthians were letters from Christ only because of Paul's love and sacrificial service on their behalf. Paul was not content to simply preach the word. His ministry was characterized by an intimate involvement in the lives of the people.

The second key concept that completes the summary of the way in which Paul measured his ministry is the results of Paul's work. Indeed, because of Paul's ministry, the fruit of the Spirit had been manifested in the lives of the saints at Corinth. Paul wrote that the Corinthians were "known and read by everybody" and that this living and breathing epistle had been "written not with ink but with the Spirit of the living God" (3:3). While Christians are not perfect (and the Corinthians certainly were not), there is an observable shift in attitude, thought, and action after one has confessed that Jesus Christ is Lord. The living letter of recommendation for Christianity is the switch from the world to Christ, from foolishness to wisdom, from works of the flesh to life in the Spirit, from hate to love. A changed life is always the best testimony.

Verse 3 contains a contrast between the Spirit and the letter written on "tablets of stone. . . ." This contrast crops up again in verse 6 and is followed by a lengthy contrast in 3:7–18 between Paul's ministry of the new covenant and the old covenant associated with his opponents. Paul held nothing back as he emphasized the superiority of the new covenant over and above the old. Paul asserted that the ministry of the Spirit is more glorious than the ministry of the law (3:7–11). Paul also said that the ministry of the old covenant is veiled, while the veil is taken away in the new covenant (3:14–16). There are vast differences between the veiled and the unveiled. The results of the old covenant that is veiled is that "their minds were made dull" (3:14) and "a veil covers their hearts" (3:15). On the other hand, the glory of the new covenant comes from the fact that "the veil is taken away" (3:16). Christians thus "reflect the Lord's glory" and "are being transformed into his likeness" (3:18). Again, the contrast between the outcomes of the old covenant and the new covenant serves as a defense of Paul's ministry. Paul's standard for ministry was the transformation of the Corinthians, which was taking place before all who had eyes to see.

A Plain and Honest Ministry (4:1–6)

In another of Paul's letters, he told the church that they should live in such a way that they so stood out from the larger culture that they would "shine like stars in the universe" (Philippians 2:14–15). Paul practiced what he preached. He conducted his ministry in such a way that people could not find any legitimate reasons to oppose his ministry. He sought to live above reproach. In 2 Corinthians 4:1–6, Paul provided a list of behaviors that could not in any way be attributed to Paul or his associates. They could not be charged with using "secret and shameful ways," and neither could they be charged with using deceptive tactics. In no way did Paul or his associates "distort the word of God." Last, in verse 5 Paul reminded the church that no one could accuse them of a self-centered ministry, "for we do not preach ourselves." That which *did* characterize Paul's ministry team was quite simple and straight-forward. They plainly proclaimed the truth that Jesus Christ is Lord, and they had humbled themselves to be the servants of all people for the sake of this Lord (2 Cor. 4:5). For Paul the simple truth was glorious enough without having to add to it. The simple truth of the gospel causes the very light of God to shine in the hearts of those who hear. It is "the light of the knowledge of the glory of God in the face of Christ" (4:6).

Perhaps it is easy for us to focus on the gap between our own ministries and that of the Apostle Paul. After all, Paul had a unique and profound salvation experience that propelled him into his calling with great enthusiasm. The power of the Spirit seems to have been available to him and the other apostles in ways that are unimaginable for us in our time here in the twenty-first century. Paul had so much going for him. Paul was so strong, while it seems we are so weak.

On the other hand, maybe the gap is not as wide as we sometimes make it out to be. To be sure, the ministry of the Apostle Paul was unique and full of excitement. However, we have been justified by the same Lord and sealed by the same Spirit (1:22). We, like Paul, are simply called to go forth and proclaim the revealed truth that Christ is Lord. As the people who have been entrusted with the ministry of reconciliation, we also are called to "[renounce] secret and shameful ways", while "commend[ing] ourselves to every man's conscience in the sight of God" (4:2).

In our culture, most people have access to many of the material needs of which the mind can conceive and then some. At the same time, most of these people recognize that something is missing.

It is truly astonishing that so often the church tries to entice visitors by offering them more of what they already have too much of in the first place: a crammed schedule, another event to write on the calendar, an emphasis on giving so that we can buy more stuff or so that we can build a family life center—so that we can host more events. This comes from a faulty way of thinking from the church's perspective, which reasons that if the pews are filled and people are busy then we must be doing a good thing. If our church is meeting its budget and doing enough stuff, then that means we're really doing ministry, right?

I am convinced that Paul would think that we measure our church's ministries by some strange and wrong-headed standards. It is saddening that pastors are put in positions where they fear for their jobs if they do not produce *results*. How different are we from the world when we fire—I mean, *dismiss*—ministers for the same reasons that big corporations dismiss their CEOs or sports' teams dismiss their head coaches? People want to attend a winning church. But what does it look like when the church is winning? What kind of results should we be looking for?

Implications and Actions

Recently our new youth minister told me that he was frustrated because he didn't feel the youth were responding.

For this reason he was tempted to focus on what seemed to excite them (games, hype, events). This led us into a serious conversation about ministry and the church.

The church should be intentional about offering people something they won't find anywhere else. People's lives are already stuffed with enough activities. Their calendars are full enough. Indeed, pastors desperately want to hold people's attention and their financial contributions. But ministers sometimes worry about the offering without giving enough consideration to what *they* are offering. Our focus as ministers and churches should be to invite people into a spiritual experience, to offer people something they will not find anywhere else. The church ought to be a place that serves as a catalyst for something meaningful to take place.

To be sure, the message of the gospel will often fall on deaf ears. However, we must be vigilant to remember that there is nothing wrong with the message. The gospel doesn't need anything added to it.

THE USE OF "WE" IN 2 CORINTHIANS

Although Paul was the one who was writing to the Corinthians, he did not forget that he was a part of a ministry team. Therefore, Paul was not only defending himself but his entire ministry team.[3] Paul's use of the plural is significant in that it shows that "he is not a maverick apostle, and his letters do not contain his peculiar opinion that stands apart from the consensus of the church. They reflect the consensus of those who are with him."[4]

CASE STUDY

A friend vents his frustration to you, saying that he has been sharing the gospel with a coworker for months. Your friend then asks you for advice on how to get the coworker to accept Christ. What advice do you give?

QUESTIONS

1. Is your church sincere about wanting people to know Christ?

2. What are the results of your church's ministry?

3. How do you know when a church function was successful?

4. What is your first reaction to the last paragraph in the *Study Guide* under "A Plain and Honest Ministry"? Do you agree with the writer? Why or why not?

NOTES —————————————————————————————

1. Unless otherwise indicated, all Scripture quotations in lessons 4–6, 9–13 are from the New International Version.

2. G.R. Beasley-Murray, "2 Corinthians," *The Broadman Bible Commentary*, vol. 11 (Nashville, Tennessee: Broadman Press, 1971), 10.

3. David Garland, "2 Corinthians," *The New American Commentary*, vol. 29 (Nashville, Tennessee: B & H Publishing Group, 1999), 50

4. Paul Barnett, "The Second Epistle to the Corinthians," *The New International Commentary on the New Testament* (Grand Rapids, Michigan: Eerdmans Publishing Company, 1997), 58.

FOCAL TEXT

2 Corinthians 4:7—5:10

BACKGROUND

2 Corinthians 4:7—5:10

LESSON TEN

View Life from Eternity

MAIN IDEA

Through God's power, we can face the challenges of life, including death, with confidence.

QUESTION TO EXPLORE

How could living from an eternal perspective of ultimate confidence in God affect your life?

STUDY AIM

To affirm God's power to help me deal with any challenge

QUICK READ

All Christians should be of good courage since God has given us the promise of eternity through Christ. Our current burdens are nothing in comparison to the glory that waits for us after this life.

A clever cat hangs around our house. In the wilds of West Texas, where rattlesnakes are plentiful and coyotes and wild hogs roam around like they own the place, the lines are sharply divided in the animal kingdom. There are many hunters and just as many hunted.

While the mice fear the newest cat that has been dropped off near our house, the cat most assuredly fears the dozens of coyotes, bobcats, and other predators that lurk around each night. But this clever cat seems well aware of the danger.

I've noticed that she's always *up*—curled *up* on top of our minivan, hanging carelessly from a lofty tree branch or someplace else *up*. On one occasion when I arrived home from a late night at the office, I met her piercing eyes staring down at me from our roof. Unlike her several unfortunate predecessors, this cat has the right idea. She recognizes that her hope is *up*. That's a pretty smart way to live.

2 CORINTHIANS 4:7–18

[7] But we have this treasure in clay jars, so that it may be made clear that this extraordinary power belongs to God and does not come from us. [8] We are afflicted in every way, but not crushed; perplexed, but not driven to despair; [9] persecuted, but not forsaken; struck down, but not destroyed; [10] always carrying in the body the death of Jesus, so that the life of Jesus may also be made visible in

our bodies. **11** For while we live, we are always being given up to death for Jesus' sake, so that the life of Jesus may be made visible in our mortal flesh. **12** So death is at work in us, but life in you.

13 But just as we have the same spirit of faith that is in accordance with scripture—"I believed, and so I spoke"—we also believe, and so we speak, **14** because we know that the one who raised the Lord Jesus will raise us also with Jesus, and will bring us with you into his presence. **15** Yes, everything is for your sake, so that grace, as it extends to more and more people, may increase thanksgiving, to the glory of God.

16 So we do not lose heart. Even though our outer nature is wasting away, our inner nature is being renewed day by day. **17** For this slight momentary affliction is preparing us for an eternal weight of glory beyond all measure, **18** because we look not at what can be seen but at what cannot be seen; for what can be seen is temporary, but what cannot be seen is eternal.

2 CORINTHIANS 5:1–10

¹For we know that if the earthly tent we live in is destroyed, we have a building from God, a house not made with hands, eternal in the heavens. **2** For in this tent we groan, longing to be clothed with our heavenly dwelling— **3** if indeed, when we have taken it off we will not be found naked. **4** For while we are still in this tent, we groan under our burden, because we wish not to be unclothed but to be further clothed, so that what is mortal may be swallowed up by life. 5 He who has prepared us for this very thing is God, who has given us the Spirit as a guarantee.

6 So we are always confident; even though we know that while we are at home in the body we are away from the Lord— 7 for we walk by faith, not by sight. 8 Yes, we do have confidence, and we would rather be away from the body and at home with the Lord. 9 So whether we are at home or away, we make it our aim to please him. 10 For all of us must appear before the judgment seat of Christ, so that each may receive recompense for what has been done in the body, whether good or evil.

The Work of Death (4:7–15)

Paul had his share of detractors in Corinth. His opponents questioned his abilities as a leader, but Paul was not hindered in the least by their criticism. On one level it might be safely said that Paul agreed with them. Using an apt metaphor, Paul described himself as a "jar of clay" (2 Corinthians 4:7)—a delicate object indeed, for dried clay shatters easily. However, one does not have to be made of iron to be in the business of ministry. This is because the real power for ministry comes not from the individual, but from God. This was why Paul could say that he and his ministry partners were "hard pressed on every side, but not crushed; perplexed, but not in despair; persecuted, but not abandoned; struck down, but not destroyed" (2 Cor. 4:8–9).

The catch is that God's care and provision are not always so easily observed. It is no secret that the Christian faith is full of paradox. Paul highlighted the paradox of his own Christian experience in verses 10 and 11. Paul served as an instrument of God to make known the life that is found in Christ (4:5–6). At the same time while Paul was busy proclaiming life in Christ, he himself was in constant danger of suffering and death. The wonderful and threatening message that Jesus proclaimed got Jesus hung on a cross. Now Paul, as a steward of this same life-giving message, must be wary of the many "dangers, toils, and snares"[1] that accompany the proclamation of such good news.

But the tables get turned yet again. Although Jesus was crucified, he was raised to new life three days later. Paul meant it when he said that there is the very real possibility of being struck down but not of being destroyed. Paul believed and would speak with confidence (4:13) in the face of his challenges because the same power that raised Christ from the dead would raise him as well (4:14). Christians, if they will lift their eyes to see it, have the benefit of an eternal perspective in the midst of challenge, hardship, and death.

Fixing Our Eyes on Eternity (4:16–18)

Paul brought chapter 4 to a close in the same way he opened it (see 4:1). "We do not lose heart," he wrote again in verse 16. Although the Corinthians might see Paul as a man who was wasting away and beaten down by life's hardships (see 11:24–28), "inwardly [he was] being renewed day by day" (4:16).

The Christian life is like a house being remodeled from the inside out. From all appearances, the place looks just as decayed as it did when the construction work began and—what's more—the place is becoming more dilapidated all the time. However, on the inside, transforming work is being performed by the Spirit that the human eye cannot see.

The old house has its walls torn down and reworked with the textures of love, kindness, and generosity. The mind is dismantled and rebuilt in order that it might contain the fullness of the wisdom of God that is found in Christ. The body is stripped of the faded groanings and desires of the flesh and replaced with the groaning will of the Spirit. Eventually, our bodies will totally and utterly decay. Life, all life, is sure to come to an end. The unrelenting combination of time, disease, and decay that batters against these "earthly tents" eventually takes its toll (5:1). However, the work that has been performed on the inside is not done in vain. For "what is unseen is eternal" (4:18).

The Work of Resurrection (5:1–10)

Just as surely as our present bodies will die, Christians can be just as sure that we will receive a new body. While no one knows exactly what will happen after we die, Paul emphasized three important things about bodily life beyond death. First, our resurrected bodies will be "from God, a house not made with hands" (5:1, NASB). Second, our resurrected bodies will be "eternal" (5:1). Third, we will be with the Lord (5:8).

The first two descriptions that Paul gives of the resurrected body go together. Our current bodies (these temporary tents) will be replaced with a "building from God" and will therefore last for eternity (5:1). When the resurrection comes, there will be no more pain, no more decay, no more death. Those things belong only to the old order of things, which will have passed away (Revelation 21:4).

In verses 2–3 Paul changed his metaphor a bit and talked of God clothing us with a new body, a "heavenly dwelling" (2 Cor. 5:2). Because of God's caring provision, Paul said "we will not be found naked" (5:3). The metaphor is beautiful and fitting. We can be sure that God, in his love and tenderness for us, will make provision for everything that we could possibly need or want. You may recall another place in the Bible where God clothed people so they would not be found naked (Genesis 3:10, 21). If God so clothed Adam and Eve in light of their sin and rebellion, how much more lavishly will God clothe the saints for their eternal stay in heaven?

This leads us into Paul's other emphasis concerning the death of Christians. When we are absent from the body, we are present with the Lord (2 Cor. 5:8). There is much mystery surrounding the subject of the afterlife, but one thing is made clear. Christians will experience the continued presence of the Lord, a conviction Paul also expressed in his Letter to the Philippians (Philippians 1:21–24). Because of this hope, we can say with Paul that "to live is Christ, and to die is gain" (Phil. 1:21).

What proof do Christians have for this outrageous claim? The Spirit that God has given us serves as proof. When people make a deposit or pledge on something, they mean serious business. The deposit indicates that they have every intention of eventually coming through with the rest of the payment. Thus, their deposit serves as a guarantee that the rest will be paid in full. This is how the Spirit functions in the context of the promises of God. Because God "has given us the Spirit as a deposit, guaranteeing what is to come" (2 Cor. 5:5), we can expect the rest to be paid in full when "what is mortal [is] swallowed up by life" (5:4), when the perishable puts on the imperishable (1 Cor. 15:53). Again, just as our hearts and minds are transformed by the work of the deposit of the Spirit, we can fully anticipate that God will pay the rest in full by transforming our bodies as well. Thus, like Paul we should "always be of good courage" (2 Cor. 5:6, 8, NASB).

This life is not all there is. This life is a very short prelude to the glory that awaits us in eternity.

Something will happen, however, between this life and eternity. Verses 9 and 10 bring this section to a close in a powerful and perhaps unsettling way. The obvious question with which we must contend is this: If we are saved by grace through faith and not by works, then just why is it that God will judge us by our works? Consider this helpful starting point for further reflection on this question. The first thing we can say with confidence is that no human being anywhere at anytime is justified by works (Romans 3:20, NASB). We can also assert that salvation is not a free pass, giving us the freedom to sin since we are saved by grace (2 Cor. 6:1–2). However, it might be helpful to view works in a different light. We can use Paul's language about the work of the Spirit in 2 Corinthians 4:16 and 5:5 as our guide. Our works are an indication of what is going on inside of us, in the "inner man" (4:16, NASB). If we are born of the Spirit of God, then that rebirth will be evident by how we live, by our deeds (James 2:14–18). Therefore, the transforming work of the Spirit will be reflected in our own works.

An analogy may be helpful. You call the plumber after you see that the water coming from your kitchen faucet is filthy. Now, when will you know that the problem has been fixed? After the plumber gets into his truck and drives away? He may be headed to town to buy parts, or to his house to fetch a much needed, but forgotten wrench.

After the plumber tells you so? He could be mistaken. The reality is that you know the problem has been fixed when, and only when, you turn on your faucet and the water comes out clean. So it is with being a Christian. You can be confident in the face of judgment when your life is characterized by the fruit of the Spirit (1 John 3:15–21). This is what Jesus was getting at when he said, "a tree is recognized by its fruit" (Matthew 12:33).

No wonder Scripture admonishes us so often to examine ourselves. For when we take a long and hard look at ourselves, we may find that we have been mistaken all along about what was really there!

Implications and Actions

We are loved and transformed by God and can say with confidence that we will also be preserved by him. While we must continue on with business as usual here on earth, we can do so with both assurance and courage.

In this life, many enemies are on the prowl. Satan indeed "prowls around like a roaring lion" (1 Peter 5:8). Besides the spiritual forces of darkness, there are other enemies to contend with as well. We live with the daily threats of doubt and insecurity that unceasingly try to slither their way into our hearts and minds. We are confronted with tragedy, illness, and death. Such difficulties sink their claws into us, and we are cut off.

For this reason we should spend as much time as we can in the high and lofty places of study, prayer, and Christian community. This is not some desperate attempt at escapism. Rather, these practices serve as sources of courage and as a reminder of the fact that our hope is *up*. Remember that your hope is *up*. It's a smart way to live.

BAPTIST MISSIONARY

In the 1700s a young shoemaker was quite good at cursing and lying. He even tried stealing, but he was caught. A little later on, he became a Christian, and he, like Paul, would come to realize that the troubles in this life were nothing compared with the glory that awaits us in eternity.

This young man went from shoemaker to preacher, missionary, linguist, and professor. In his lifetime, he launched a missionary movement, translated the Bible into forty languages, and spent his life preaching to and establishing schools for the people in India. That's not all! He also lost two wives and a child. He was slandered. Through much of his life, he was in danger. He was often lonely and sometimes severely depressed, and was no stranger to poverty. His name was William Carey, also known as the father of modern missions.[2]

APPLYING THIS LESSON TO LIFE

- Ask God for the courage to identify the fears in your life.

- Develop the habit of asking this question: *How big of a deal is this going to be in eternity?*

- Make it your goal to please God.

- Take time to evaluate your life. Identify the things in your life with which God would be pleased as well as those things God would not like. Pray for God to give you the strength to overcome your sin and weaknesses.

QUESTIONS

1. Is there anything in life that causes you to lose heart? Based on this lesson's Scripture, can you imagine what the Apostle Paul might say to you?

2. Paul spoke of both *faith* and *knowing* in the same breath (2 Cor. 4:13–14). What are those things that your *faith* has caused you to *know*?

3. In what ways have you grown since you first accepted Christ?

4. How clear is the water coming out of your faucet?

N O T E S

1. "Amazing Grace," words by John Newton (1725–1807).
2. See Timothy George, *Faithful Witness: The Life and Mission of William Carey* (Birmingham: New Hope, 1991).

LESSON ELEVEN

Get Motivated to Minister

MAIN IDEA

What God has done for us in reconciling us to himself in Christ should be more than sufficient to motivate us to minister.

QUESTION TO EXPLORE

What does it take to get you motivated?

STUDY AIM

To lead adults to decide on ways they will respond to God's motivations to ministry

QUICK READ

Do Christians need to be motivated to minister? If so, what motivates you to minister to the people in your world?

I once worked with two men, each of whom kept an important picture on his desk. Like many men and women, one had a picture of his son, whom he loved with all of his heart. The other had a picture of a boat, the object of his dreams. The first man kept his son before him as a reminder that he was working for something bigger than himself: his family. The second man kept a picture of a boat as a goal to work hard so he could earn more money and be able to buy the boat he wanted. Each had found motivation to work, good or bad, important or not. Ironically, the second man had neither a family nor a boat, but the first had both a family and a boat.

Motivation is the directed desire to accomplish something. Motivation is a good thing, compelling us to act and to be passionate. It keeps us from slipping into ruts or from giving up. It defines purpose in our lives—in our families, our careers, our accomplishments, and even our churches. Each Christian should be motivated to be a minister for the Lord and not leave the work of the church for the paid staff.

2 CORINTHIANS 5:11–21

[11] Therefore, knowing the fear of the Lord, we try to persuade others; but we ourselves are well known to God, and I hope that we are also well known to your consciences. [12] We are not commending ourselves to you again, but

giving you an opportunity to boast about us, so that you may be able to answer those who boast in outward appearance and not in the heart. [13] For if we are beside ourselves, it is for God; if we are in our right mind, it is for you. [14] For the love of Christ urges us on, because we are convinced that one has died for all; therefore all have died. [15] And he died for all, so that those who live might live no longer for themselves, but for him who died and was raised for them.

[16] From now on, therefore, we regard no one from a human point of view; even though we once knew Christ from a human point of view, we know him no longer in that way. [17] So if anyone is in Christ, there is a new creation: everything old has passed away; see, everything has become new! [18] All this is from God, who reconciled us to himself through Christ, and has given us the ministry of reconciliation; [19] that is, in Christ God was reconciling the world to himself, not counting their trespasses against them, and entrusting the message of reconciliation to us. [20] So we are ambassadors for Christ, since God is making his appeal through us; we entreat you on behalf of Christ, be reconciled to God. [21] For our sake he made him to be sin who knew no sin, so that in him we might become the righteousness of God.

2 CORINTHIANS 6:1–2

[1] As we work together with him, we urge you also not to accept the grace of God in vain. [2] For he says,

"At an acceptable time I have listened to you,
and on a day of salvation I have helped you."
See, now is the acceptable time; see, now is the day of
salvation!

The Fear of the Lord (5:11–13)

The "fear of the Lord" is often misunderstood or over-looked. The phrase often brings up images of a judgmental, angry God, not the picture of God many contemporary Christians care to think about.

Fear (Greek, *phobos*) is often understood as *reverence, respect,* or *awe.* Although these are part of its meaning, *fear* is primarily understood in biblical terms as *fright* or *alarm.* "Fear of the Lord" should be understood as a combination of the two: (1) meaning to respect and revere the Lord but (2) also meaning that God is an awesome and powerful God who will bring judgment. We can be certain of the latter meaning in 2 Corinthians 5:11 because it follows verse 10, which says that "we must all appear before the judgment seat of Christ." Christians must be careful not to water down the gospel so that we miss the point that a righteous God will not allow sin in his kingdom and that we will all be held accountable before God (Romans 14:12).

Although salvation is a free, gracious gift from God, an appropriate "fear of the Lord" should motivate us to serve

Christ and to lead those who stand in judgment to turn to Christ. Paul wrote in his earlier letter to the Corinthians that our works of service will be either gold, silver, costly stones, wood, hay, or straw. We will all be judged as through fire, either refining our works or devouring them (1 Corinthians 3:10–15). We should rest in confidence that God loves us with a gracious and covenantal love, but God is also an awesome and powerful God who does not want us to lead sinful lives. God is more interested in "what is in the heart" than "what is seen" (2 Cor. 5:12).

The Love of Christ (5:14–15)

"Christ's love" is an even greater motivation than the "fear of the Lord." Paul said that the love of Christ "compels" us to minister. Both of these motivations reveal an aspect of the work of Christ. Fear of the Lord is based on the fact that Christ is our Judge (5:10). Love is based on the fact that Christ is our Savior (5:14). He "died for all." "All" means every one of us, even those who had no affection for him. Romans 5:6 says, "Christ died for the ungodly." Romans 5:8 adds, "while we were still sinners, Christ died for us." His death is available to all, but that does not mean that all people are saved. Only those who believe in him are actually saved. John 3:16 and Romans 10:9 remind us that salvation comes through belief in and acceptance of Christ's sacrificial death.

The love of Christ was demonstrated by his coming and death for us. We died with Christ when he died, meaning that the consequence of our sin died with him. We should then live for him in such a way that the world sees Jesus reflected in our actions and attitudes. How disappointing it must be to Jesus when we do not love others as we should after he has shown us so much love. John tells us, "This is how we know what love is: Jesus Christ laid down his life for us. And we ought to lay down our lives for our brothers" (1 John 3:16), and "Dear friends, let us love one another, for love comes from God. Everyone who loves has been born of God and knows God" (1 John 4:7). Lovingly ministering to others is part of what it means to be a Christian.

Being a New Creation in Christ (5:16–21)

Being "a new creation" is a third motivation for ministry. We are changed by God for a purpose. We are no longer the "ungodly" sinners mentioned in Romans 5:6, but we are reconciled to God (2 Cor. 5:18). This reconciliation develops within us a new life. As 2 Corinthians 5:17 says, "The old has gone, the new has come!" Being a new creation in Christ changes our vision; we no longer see with a "worldly point of view" (5:16), but with a Christlike vision. When we regard others as Jesus does, we do not see their frail human condition, but we see them as

God's children who need love, mercy, or grace. Once Paul establishes that we are each a new creation, he gives us two commands: we are to be ministers of reconciliation, and we are to be ambassadors of Christ.

Being a new creation is not an end unto itself. We are made new for the purpose of leading others to God. Second Corinthians 5:18 records the fact of God's reconciliation of us, the way God reconciled, and the purpose for which God reconciled us. The biblical understanding of reconciliation is to be in a perfectly restored relationship.

The Bible is the story of community, fellowship, and relationship. God created us for fellowship with him. By sinning, we disrupt that fellowship and break the relationship. We do this with God and also with other people. Sin leads to broken fellowship and ultimately destroys community. God's plan throughout Scripture is to restore community, first between him and us, and then among the community of his people, the church. Salvation is the restoration of relationship with God. God reconciled us because he loves us.

Second Corinthians 5:18 says that God reconciled us for the purpose of serving him in the ministry of reconciliation. The practical application of this ministry is threefold. First, we must first be at peace with God. Second, based on our experience with God, we must be peacemakers with those who have wronged us. Sometimes that means we must take the initiative. We must also be peacemakers with those whom we have wronged (intentionally or not). It is not good enough for Christians who have been reconciled to God to ignore the broken relationships in their lives. As much as each of us can, we need to make serious attempts to reconcile with all people. Sometimes our attempts are not accepted, but we should try regardless of the wrongs that occurred. We must forgive like God, who did not count "men's sins against them" (5:19). Third, a big part of our ministry of reconciliation is to lead other people to God, individuals who have broken lives or who are far from God. Paul gave his life to lead others to Christ. We are commissioned to do the same (5:18).

Being a new creation also leads us to another role. We are ambassadors of Christ. Ambassadors are representatives of one nation or kingdom to another. For example, the ambassador from the United States to China lives in China but is a resident of the United States. Paul was making this precise point. We are not *of* this world, and yet we are still *in* the world. By serving as ambassadors of Christ, we are still in this world but representatives of another realm, the kingdom of God. The transfer of citizenship from this world to the kingdom of God happened in the moment of reconciliation, in the moment we became a new creation, for the old has been removed. As ambassadors, we have the responsibility to represent our gracious Savior to the world around us. We should carry the message of reconciliation with us wherever we go.

The Urgency of Time (6:1–2)

The final motivation for ministry is the urgency of time. "Now is the time of God's favor, now is the day of salvation" (6:2). The time is urgent because of one of two reasons. Either Jesus will return soon, or one by one each of us will enter into his presence soon. Either way, we ought to be motivated. The time is indeed short. The time to be reconciled to God is now! The time to be reconciled to others is now! The time to lead others to be reconciled to God is now! As we regard others with a heavenly point of view, let us remember that this life is temporary but the one to come is eternal.

In light of how short life is, Paul wrote that we are not only commissioned to a ministry of reconciliation by God but also that we are actually co-workers with God (6:1). God loves us so much that he not only reconciled us but also calls us to minister to others. We are "God's fellow workers" (6:1). Let us consider those in our lives who need reconciliation now. Let us act as fellow workers with God to reconcile them to us and ultimately to God.

Implications and Actions

There are many motivations for Christians to serve others. What is yours—fear, love, a renewed life, an urgency of limited time, or something else? Consider what God has done for you, and then seek how you can help others. Ministering to others should be a natural extension of our relationship with Christ. How can we minister in practical ways? Are we paying attention enough to know what needs exist around us?

God reconciled us to himself. Have you experienced that reconciliation? How can you lead others to do the same? We have been given a ministry and a message of reconciliation. Let us take seriously these responsibilities as we minister to the world around us.

In Christ

The phrase "in Christ" (2 Cor. 5:17) and its alternatives *in Christ Jesus* and *in the Lord* are commonly used by Paul. The expressions apply to the state of Christians in relationship to Jesus Christ. The phrase identifies the inclusive oneness of all Christians as a unit while setting Christians apart from the rest of the world as exclusively distinct. "In Christ" defines the church as one community of faith in union with Jesus Christ. We share in the person, the work, and the characteristics of Jesus.

"In Christ" defines a corporate personality of all of the followers of Jesus. Although Paul used the phrase "in Christ Jesus," he never used "in Jesus," demonstrating that the phrase focuses on the messiahship of Jesus and not his humanity.

MINISTERING IN THE LOVE OF CHRIST

What are some practical ways you can show the love of Christ?

- To a family member or a friend who has lost a job

- To someone dealing with a serious health issue

- To a couple struggling in their marriage

- To someone overwhelmed with financial difficulties

- To a minister who seems overloaded

- To a divided community (an office, a church, a family, a school)

QUESTIONS

1. In light of Romans 14:12; 1 Corinthians 3:10–15; and 2 Corinthians 5:10, how seriously do you take the "fear of the Lord'? Or is that a part of Christianity you would rather not think about?

2. Would you say that you are a "new creation?" Are you restored in your relationship with God?

3. How can you be a minister of reconciliation in your home, work, or community?

4. How are you an ambassador of Christ?

5. What urgency do you feel to lead others to God?

FOCAL TEXT

2 Corinthians 8:1–15;
9:7–8, 11–15

BACKGROUND

2 Corinthians 8—9

LESSON TWELVE

Become Generous in Giving

Compelling reasons call us to decide to give generously of our financial resources to the Lord's work.

How well does your financial giving match New Testament teachings?

To outline Paul's teachings about giving financially and to decide to give generously to the Lord's work

Paul provides examples and instructions for giving generously to the Lord's work with the right attitude.

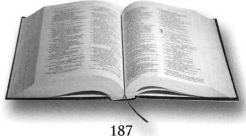

It seems like everyone is always asking for money, even at church. What does the Bible say about how Christians are to give?

2 CORINTHIANS 8:1–15

[1] We want you to know, brothers and sisters, about the grace of God that has been granted to the churches of Macedonia; [2] for during a severe ordeal of affliction, their abundant joy and their extreme poverty have overflowed in a wealth of generosity on their part. [3] For, as I can testify, they voluntarily gave according to their means, and even beyond their means, [4] begging us earnestly for the privilege of sharing in this ministry to the saints— [5] and this, not merely as we expected; they gave themselves first to the Lord and, by the will of God, to us, [6] so that we might urge Titus that, as he had already made a beginning, so he should also complete this generous undertaking among you. [7] Now as you excel in everything—in faith, in speech, in knowledge, in utmost eagerness, and in our love for you—so we want you to excel also in this generous undertaking.

[8] I do not say this as a command, but I am testing the genuineness of your love against the earnestness of others. [9] For you know the generous act of our Lord Jesus Christ, that though he was rich, yet for your sakes he became poor, so that by his poverty you might become rich. [10] And in

this matter I am giving my advice: it is appropriate for you who began last year not only to do something but even to desire to do something— ¹¹ now finish doing it, so that your eagerness may be matched by completing it according to your means. ¹² For if the eagerness is there, the gift is acceptable according to what one has—not according to what one does not have. ¹³ I do not mean that there should be relief for others and pressure on you, but it is a question of a fair balance between ¹⁴ your present abundance and their need, so that their abundance may be for your need, in order that there may be a fair balance. ¹⁵ As it is written,

"The one who had much did not have too much,
    and the one who had little did not have too little."

2 CORINTHIANS 9:7–8, 11–15

⁷ Each of you must give as you have made up your mind, not reluctantly or under compulsion, for God loves a cheerful giver. ⁸ And God is able to provide you with every blessing in abundance, so that by always having enough of everything, you may share abundantly in every good work.

• • • • • • • • • • • • • • • • • • •

¹¹ You will be enriched in every way for your great generosity, which will produce thanksgiving to God through us; ¹² for the rendering of this ministry not only supplies the needs of the saints but also overflows with many

thanksgivings to God. [13] Through the testing of this ministry you glorify God by your obedience to the confession of the gospel of Christ and by the generosity of your sharing with them and with all others, [14] while they long for you and pray for you because of the surpassing grace of God that he has given you. [15] Thanks be to God for his indescribable gift!

Giving Is an Act of Grace (8:1–9)

God is a giver. God gave the gift of his Son, Jesus. God gave us the gift of the gospel. God gave us the gift of the Holy Spirit. He gave us the church. Each of these gifts is an evidence of God's grace toward us. Consequently, we are more like God when we demonstrate love through giving than just about any other time. Giving is a wonderful privilege.

Paul gave two examples of giving: the example of the Macedonians (2 Corinthians 8:1–7) and the example of Christ himself (2 Cor. 8:8–9). The churches of Macedonia were the churches in Philippi, Thessalonica, and Berea. They gave "out of the most severe trial" (8:2). Other Scriptures about these churches mention words like *severe suffering* and *persecution* (see Philippians 1:29–30; 1 Thessalonians 1:6; 2:14; 3:3–4). Often we withdraw from helping others when things become challenging. We do this as individuals and even as churches. We begin to think about our own needs (and rightfully so), but we go too far. We think of our needs to the exclusion of the needs of others. Paul reminded the Corinthians, a wealthy church, that the Macedonian churches did not withdraw into themselves when they were suffering; instead they chose to give of what they had to help others. In a day of economic strain and challenge, we must not forget that there are others in need. Let us give even if we are suffering or if we are going through difficulties ourselves.

The Macedonian churches also gave out of their meager possessions. Paul said they even gave out of their extreme poverty (2 Cor. 8:2). We make excuses about why we are not able to give, but most of us do not live in "extreme poverty." Many of us can list luxuries and wants that we choose for ourselves over participating in God's grace of giving. The Macedonians did not give out of their abundance, but "beyond their ability." The only thing they had that was "overflowing" was their joy. How many Christians seem to have these priorities switched! Even though many people have an abundance of things, they seem to lack real joy.

God was a giver, and God called us to be like him. Since we are meant to be givers, we are not living out what our Christian spirit demands if we do not give. We rob ourselves of the experience of the joy in the grace of giving.

The Macedonian churches gave voluntarily, "entirely on their own" (8:3–4). They even urgently pleaded for the "privilege" (from the same Greek root word as *grace*) of sharing. Paul was having to remind the wealthy church in Corinth to be generous with what they had while the poor, persecuted churches in Macedonia were looking for places to give. Giving to God and God's work was a part of who they were. They gave eagerly, without excuse and even without prodding. Giving was natural for them because they had given themselves to the Lord completely (8:5). Now Paul was asking the Corinthians to complete this act of grace as the Macedonian churches had done. It is not enough to want to give or even to start to give. We must finish the work of giving that God has called us to do.

The Corinthians excelled in other gifts but fell short in this one. Christians may think that as long as they are fine in one area, their shortcomings in other areas will not matter as much. Even if we are strong in other areas of our faith, let also us excel in the grace of giving (8:7).

The second example of giving as an act of grace is Christ (8:8–9). Jesus, as King of heaven, was rich but gave that up and became poor for our sake. He showed us how to live out the act of grace. He was willing to lay down his life for us, and in turn we must be willing to follow him, not longing after the things of this world.

Be Faithful in Giving (8:10–15)

As mentioned before, faithfulness in giving is completing the act of grace. The Corinthian church was the first in desire to give but not actually first to complete its giving (8:10–11). In fact, they still had not finished their commitment. It should be natural for Christians to have the desire to give to the Lord, but we must have the discipline to actually follow through on our desire. How many programs and ministries have not achieved what God had for them because of gifts that were never given? What ministries at your church or in your community are starving right now from unfulfilled commitments?

Giving is measured by the heart not the pocketbook. Some can give very little, but their service means more to God than that of people who may give large sums. We are to give according to our means, according to what we have (8:11–12). Notice that Paul did not mention the amount the Macedonians gave but that they gave out of their poverty. The Corinthians were far wealthier but had failed to give what they promised. Wealth is not the foundation of giving; rather, a real desire is. Today, perhaps some people who have plenty of income have been weighed down by debt and commitment, and their high income does not lead to high giving to God. The priority of the heart is revealed by where our money goes.

Biblical giving includes equality and caring for those in need. We are to be a blessing to others when we are in plenty (8:14). We are part of a community together. We should be concerned about the gospel being spread and about taking care of the needs of others. Jesus called us to care about the needs of others (see Matthew 25:31–46).

Give with the Right Attitude (9:7–8, 11–15)

We can give in a wrong way and in a right way. Notice that in these verses the amount of the gift is never mentioned but the motivation behind the gift is important. Paul referred to three right attitudes each giver should have as he or she presents a gift to God. He started by listing two wrong attitudes (although these are not the only wrong ones): giving reluctantly and giving out of obligation (2 Cor. 9:7).

Learning the discipline of giving to God can be hard for some people, especially at first. If we are not careful, we can think of all of the things the money could have bought. We must not become reluctant givers. God was not a reluctant giver. He gave his only Son, Jesus, who then gave his life for us. Likewise, let us not give out of obligation ("under compulsion") alone. Doing so would make giving a work of the law instead of a work of grace. We are not bound by the law, but we are freed by grace.

Paul gave three better attitudes for giving to the Lord than out of a sense of obligation: give cheerfully, generously, and thankfully. In contrast to reluctance, Christian giving must be cheerful (9:7). We give cheerfully because we are giving to an important purpose, the work of God. Giving cheerfully is evidence of where our hearts are. Either our hearts are turned toward the things of God or they are not. If we are engaged in God's kingdom work, then we will eagerly and cheerfully give of our time, talents, energy, and resources to God and God's work. If our hearts are focused on the things of this world, our giving (if we give at all) will be hesitant, reluctant, meager, or regretful. Are you an eager giver or a meager giver? "God loves a cheerful giver" (9:7).

Generosity is the second attitude of giving mentioned in this section. Second Corinthians 9:9 says that God has "scattered abroad his gifts" as evidence of the broadness and the amount of God's generosity. Paul mentioned giving generously six times in chapter 9 (9:5, 6, 11, 13). Generosity ought to be a characteristic of every Christian. There is a benefit to generosity. The giver as well as the receiver is blessed. Proverbs 11:25 says, "A generous man will prosper; he who refreshes others will himself be refreshed." Proverbs 22:9 adds, "A generous man will himself be blessed, for he shares his food with the poor." Prosperity, blessing, and a refreshed soul come to those who have the spirit of generosity. We cannot outgive God.

The third attitude we should have is thankfulness. Second Corinthians 9:11, 15 mention thanks as a part of giving. Giving to the Lord is the most appropriate way to demonstrate our gratitude for what God has done for us. The offering itself is an expression of thanks to God. We give out of what we already have. We should acknowledge that all comes from God and that it all really belongs to him. We are only stewards of what God has given to us. By returning a portion of what God has provided, we are demonstrating that all belongs to God. Giving to the Lord's work brings God praise when others are blessed by our gift. The recipients will have reason to thank God. In essence, giving can be an opportunity to bring a double praise to God. The act itself is a praise of thanks, and the end result will bring a praise of thanks. Many cultures have set aside a day or time of thanksgiving. As Christians, do we appropriately offer thanks to God? Do we forget to give thanks to God for "his indescribable gift" of Jesus (9:15)?

Implications and Actions

The Bible is clear that we are to give and that we are to have the right attitude when giving. Even so, many Christians struggle with faithfulness in giving. Why? Many simply have not set the right priorities in life.

Today's generation of Christians is one of the wealthiest the world has ever known, and yet many people are committed to a lifestyle that has financially pinched the Lord out of their budget. We are supposed to be responsible for our financial commitments, but we must consider first the tithe before making such commitments.

WHERE IN THE BIBLE DOES IT SAY TO GIVE TEN PERCENT?

The word *tithe* means a tenth, that portion of income set aside for God and his work. The first mention of a tithe given to God is by Abraham (Genesis 14:18–20), who gave to Melchizedek (God's representative). Likewise Jacob gave a tithe (Gen. 28:22), but his was given directly to the Lord.

The command to tithe is found in Numbers 18:20–32 and Deuteronomy 14:22–29. The people of Israel were to set aside a tithe (one tenth) of their income for the work of the Lord and to support the Levites (the priests). They were actually to set aside an additional tithe every third year to take care of the neediest in their communities—the orphans, widows, and foreigners. Jesus said that we should be sure to add justice, mercy, and faithfulness to tithing (Matt. 23:23; Luke 11:42).

UNWANTED TITHES

Although we are commanded to give, the Lord has the right to refuse our gifts. Amos 4—5 tells us that God refused the gifts from his people because of the injustices they were causing or allowing to happen. Acts 5 tells the story of Ananias and Sapphira, who gave a great deal to God but were punished because they exaggerated the amount. God wants us to give, but he wants us to be sure that we are right in the other areas of our lives so that our gifts will be found worthy.

QUESTIONS

1. How is giving an act of grace?

2. Are you faithful in giving to the Lord? Why or why not?

3. Is there anything you need to change about the way you budget and spend your income so you can place priority on giving to the Lord on a more regular basis?

4. If you do give faithfully, do you give with the right attitude: cheerfully, generously, and thankfully?

5. Will you make the commitment to be responsible before the Lord with your money, either continuing to do so or starting to do so today?

FOCAL TEXT

2 Corinthians 12:1–10

BACKGROUND

2 Corinthians 10:1—13:13

LESSON THIRTEEN

Rely On God's Grace

MAIN IDEA

Our greatest strength comes from relying on God's grace rather than on our accomplishments.

QUESTION TO EXPLORE

Do we dare to rely on God's grace rather than our accomplishments?

STUDY AIM

To state why Paul found God's grace sufficient in dealing with difficulty and to identify experiences in which I have found God's grace, not my strength, to be sufficient

QUICK READ

Paul tells us that there is purpose in suffering: to demonstrate the sufficiency of God's grace.

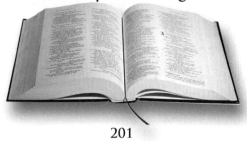

Everyone has highs and lows in life. Paul certainly did. How he handled the difficulties he faced can offer us help in dealing with our own difficulties.

The concluding four chapters of 2 Corinthians read like a roller coaster. Paul wrote about the highs and lows of ministry in general and the highs and lows of his own personal life. He listed what God had accomplished through him as well as his unique spiritual experiences. He also detailed some of the suffering he had endured for the cause of Christ. Ultimately, he exalted the greatness of God's grace.

In chapter 10, Paul addressed his own apostleship. The charge had been made that as an apostle, Paul was insufficient in some way. He sarcastically referred to those who put him down as "super-apostles" (2 Corinthians 11:5; 12:11). Paul was defending himself against the charges that he was not the same in person as he was in absence, that he was "timid" while face to face but "bold" when away (2 Cor. 10:1, see also 10:10; 13:10). Paul was balancing personal grace and humility with his influence and his authority. He constantly went back and forth between his rights as the Corinthians' spiritual parent (12:14) and his desire to serve them (12:15). Paul was forced to validate his ministry by "boasting" of his role as their apostle (12:1).

In chapter 11, Paul then contrasted his role with those whom he called "super-apostles" (11:5) but who were really "false apostles" (11:13). They selfishly used their credentials to elevate themselves and to be served by the people of Corinth. Paul used his credentials to elevate God and so that he could serve the Corinthians.

The charge may have been made that Paul was handing out foolishness or that he was a fool. Although this would have been a serious charge, it fits the disparaging attacks made by these false apostles. He referred to himself as a fool five times (11:1, 16, 21; 12:6, 11), but he embraced the term as a platform of "boasting" in the Lord. He exalted himself only to the point that he was equal to any other person who would claim authority of apostleship. He was not boasting out of pride for self-serving purposes but to establish his rightful place of authority. But in doing so, he switched back and forth from "boasting" to calling himself a "fool."

Paul talked about the privileges of being an apostle, but also the suffering he had had to endure. He shared that he had seen great spiritual visions but that God had allowed a thorn to remain in his flesh. His roller coaster ends with him saying that he continually lived with his own weakness but in God's power.

2 CORINTHIANS 12:1–10

¹ It is necessary to boast; nothing is to be gained by it, but I will go on to visions and revelations of the Lord. ² I know a person in Christ who fourteen years ago was caught up to

the third heaven—whether in the body or out of the body I do not know; God knows. ³ And I know that such a person—whether in the body or out of the body I do not know; God knows— ⁴ was caught up into Paradise and heard things that are not to be told, that no mortal is permitted to repeat. ⁵ On behalf of such a one I will boast, but on my own behalf I will not boast, except of my weaknesses. ⁶ But if I wish to boast, I will not be a fool, for I will be speaking the truth. But I refrain from it, so that no one may think better of me than what is seen in me or heard from me, ⁷ even considering the exceptional character of the revelations. Therefore, to keep me from being too elated, a thorn was given me in the flesh, a messenger of Satan to torment me, to keep me from being too elated. ⁸ Three times I appealed to the Lord about this, that it would leave me, ⁹ but he said to me, "My grace is sufficient for you, for power is made perfect in weakness." So, I will boast all the more gladly of my weaknesses, so that the power of Christ may dwell in me. ¹⁰ Therefore I am content with weaknesses, insults, hardships, persecutions, and calamities for the sake of Christ; for whenever I am weak, then I am strong.

Rely On God's Grace While Receiving Privileges from God (12:1–6)

Paul continued "boasting" to establish his authority by sharing about his experience of being caught up before the

Lord. He spoke in third person to lessen the appearance of bragging. He used the same Greek word *harpagenta* that he used in 1 Thessalonians 4:17 to refer to the end-time rapture of the church. It means *grabbed* or *snatched*. The emphasis is not on the one taken but on the act itself or even more importantly on the one who does the *snatching*: God.

In defense of his ministry Paul was speaking of the privilege of being given special visions and revelations. He was nullifying the accusations that he was not a real apostle, but in doing so, he still remained humble in spirit. He said that he was "caught up to the third heaven" (2 Cor. 12:2) and also to "paradise" (12:4). Consider three possible meanings of these two events: (1) They are one and the same, and Paul just repeated himself. (2) They are two completely separate events at separate times. (3) They are one event that includes two levels of risings (like a telescope). Many in the Jewish world at this time considered heaven as having multiple levels. Paul assumed as much and stated that he was taken into the third level.

Whether Paul was caught up to heaven once or twice (or even more) is beside the point. Paul was exceedingly qualified as an apostle, and yet he regarded the privilege not as a reward or self-serving credential but as a work of grace. He did not flaunt it or even fully explain it. Like the other privileges he had in serving God, he chose to demonstrate humility. He acknowledged that they were acts of God's grace toward him. Visions and revelations of God and heaven would certainly give Paul reason to boast, but he chose to boast not of himself but of God and God's grace. Likewise, we have been given many privileges in Christ. Let us use them not as self-honoring but as a means of serving others.

Rely On God's Grace While Enduring Suffering for God (12:7–8)

Paul went back and forth from "boasting" to demonstrating humility. He was careful to establish his apostolic credentials but also to show his humanity. After talking about this unusual and special spiritual activity of being caught up to heaven, he quickly brought himself down to earth by mentioning his "thorn in the flesh."

Just as Paul left his heavenly experience vague, he gave little details of his "thorn." It seems probable that it was a physical issue. Paul listed the physical sufferings he had to endure as a result of his apostleship: prison, floggings, beatings, stoning, various dangers, hunger and such (11:23–28). Undoubtedly, these would have caused severe physical trauma. He must have had broken bones, torn skin, lacerated muscles, and injury to internal organs through them all. Some of these might have healed completely while others might have not healed very well. Any of them could have been a "thorn" in his body. Yet it was his illness that led him to begin his ministry to the

Galatians (Galatians 4:13–14). Some suggest that Galatians 6:11 hints that Paul might have had poor vision, "see what large letters I use as I write to you with my own hand," or perhaps he had trouble writing altogether (which would make sense from the beating and stoning, not to mention any possible natural ailments like arthritis). Paul used other people to write his letters (for example, see Romans 16:22). He added only a line or two as evidence of his authorship (1 Corinthians 16:21; Colossians 4:18; 2 Thessalonians 3:17).

Perhaps the "thorn" was something spiritual, or maybe it had nothing to do with Paul at all but referred to the false apostles who were attacking Paul. Regardless of what it was, God did not remove it from him. Paul "pleaded" three times, but God did not remove it. Paul called the thorn a "messenger of Satan" and that it "torments" him, but still God did not remove it. These verses settle a false belief that continues in contemporary Christianity, that God wants only blessings for his people, and that we suffer only as a result of a lack of faith, prayer, or obedience. On the contrary, God allowed Paul to suffer, not only with the thorn but the entire list of tragedies found in 2 Corinthians 11, despite his faith, prayers, and obedience. God allowed him to suffer so he could experience something more powerful: God's grace!

I am glad Paul did not reveal what his weakness was because the ambiguity allows us all to know that we are not alone in our weaknesses, whether they are physical, emotional, spiritual, or whatever. Regardless of what our individual weaknesses are, we can follow Paul's example as we turn them over to God and rely on God's grace to help us.

Rely On God's Perfectly Sufficient Grace (12:9–10)

Paul has led us through his struggles with boasting and suffering while always giving glory to God and keeping a spirit of humility. Now he gives us the remedy that his soul needed the most: the answer he received from God, "My grace is sufficient for you." The sufficiency of grace can carry us through sorrow or deliver us from it. Grace overpowers our weakness, or it supplies us strength in our weaknesses. The power of the light bulb is more glorious in utter darkness than in the middle of the day. Likewise, Paul wrote that the power of God is made perfect in our weakness. The more we seem helpless, the greater the help is from God. We should "delight in weaknesses, in insults, in hardships, in persecutions, in difficulties" (12:10) because in them we are made strong by the power of God.

Paul did not say this lightly. Remember the hardships from chapter 11 that he suffered for the sake of Christ (11:23–33). He knew suffering, but he could see that God had a bigger purpose. God uses our suffering to make us better, or perhaps God uses our suffering to benefit others in his kingdom.

We need to see beyond our immediate situations to envision how God can use even hardships for God's good in our lives. Perhaps we even need to see beyond ourselves to imagine how God will use our difficulties in the lives of other people. As Paul wrote in Romans 8:28, "And we know that in all things God works for the good of those who love him, who have been called according to his purpose." Notice that this verse does not say that God causes everything to happen. God does not cause everything to happen, but God does allow all things, even bad, like Paul's "thorn." The Apostle knew that God had a way of redeeming even those things we do not like for a greater good.

Implications and Actions

God is at work in the lives of all of us. At times we see the blessings God's grace brings, and at other times we see how God's grace sustains us in times of suffering. Whether we are experiencing the excitement of visions and revelations or having to endure the hardships and insults, let us find our strength in the Lord.

Paul gloried in his weakness because he realized that God's power would shine in his weakness. He boasted gladly about them (2 Cor. 12:9), so that it would be evident that the power of Christ would carry him.

Sometimes we belittle our weaknesses, hoping to make ourselves look better to those around us. We answer the question of how we are doing with a simple *fine* when things are really not all that fine but we are afraid of what others will think. We do not want to appear vulnerable. This is especially true for Christian leaders. Paul debunked this form of thinking. He freely admitted he had his own weaknesses (whatever they were). Let us admit to ourselves, to others, and most importantly to God that we cannot handle the "thorns" of this life without the help of God's grace.

HEAVEN (PARADISE)

Paradise was a word that the Hebrews borrowed from the Persians. It means *garden* or *park*. It is interchangeable with *heaven*.

Paul had a lot to say about heaven. It is where the angels live (Galatians 1:8). It is where Jesus came from (Ephesians 4:9; Romans 10:6), where Jesus returned (Eph. 4:10; 6:9; Col. 4:1, Rom. 8:34), and from where Jesus will come to earth again (Philippians 3:20; 1 Thess. 1:10; 4:16; 2 Thess. 1:7). Heaven is the eternal home of Christians (2 Cor. 5:1–2).

Heaven is certainly a reality, not only for the life to come but a place we can have interaction with now in the Spirit and through prayers. It is not just a futuristic reward. Ephesians 2:6 says that we are seated with Christ in heaven now. In Christ, we have representation in heaven, and we hold a deposit for that which is fully to come.

PRIVILEGES OF GOD'S GRACE

Do you think of the following items as God's gifts of grace? How can you use them to honor God and not self?

- Wealth

- Intelligence (including deep knowledge of the Bible)

- Eloquence in speaking or teaching

- High position in the church; leadership

- Confidence of others

- Spiritual discernment

- Talent in music or the arts

QUESTIONS

1. When it comes to your successes, are you more interested in receiving credit and glory or do you give all credit to God (and not with false modesty)?

2. What privileges has God given you? Are you faithful in serving him?

3. What does the hope of heaven mean for those who are suffering now?

4. What are some "thorns" in your flesh that you would like removed? Can you imagine how God can bring them to good?

5. Can you look back and see how God's grace sustained you through difficult times?

6. In what experiences have you found strength in God's grace?

Our Next New Study
(Available for use beginning December 2011)

THE GOSPEL OF MATTHEW:
A Primer for Discipleship

UNIT THREE. FURTHER INSTRUCTIONS ON GENUINE DISCIPLESHIP

UNIT FOUR. FOLLOWING JESUS' COMMAND

Additional Future Adult Study

How to Order More Bible Study Materials

It's easy! Just fill in the following information. For additional Bible study materials available both in print and online, see www.baptistwaypress.org, or get a complete order form of available print materials—including Spanish materials—by calling 1-866-249-1799 or e-mailing baptistway@texasbaptists.org.

Title of item	Price	Quantity	Cost
This Issue:			
The Corinthian Letters—Study Guide (BWP001121)	$3.55	_____	_____
The Corinthian Letters—Large Print Study Guide (BWP001122)	$4.25	_____	_____
The Corinthian Letters—Teaching Guide (BWP001123)	$4.95	_____	_____
Additional Issues Available:			
Growing Together in Christ—Study Guide (BWP001036)	$3.25	_____	_____
Growing Together in Christ—Teaching Guide (BWP001038)	$3.75	_____	_____
Living Faith in Daily Life—Study Guide (BWP001095)	$3.55	_____	_____
Living Faith in Daily Life—Large Print Study Guide (BWP001096)	$3.95	_____	_____
Living Faith in Daily Life—Teaching Guide (BWP001097)	$4.25	_____	_____
Participating in God's Mission—Study Guide (BWP001077)	$3.55	_____	_____
Participating in God's Mission—Large Print Study Guide (BWP001078)	$3.95	_____	_____
Participating in God's Mission—Teaching Guide (BWP001079)	$3.95	_____	_____
Profiles in Character—Study Guide (BWP001112)	$3.55	_____	_____
Profiles in Character—Large Print Study Guide (BWP001113)	$4.25	_____	_____
Profiles in Character—Teaching Guide (BWP001114)	$4.95	_____	_____
Genesis: People Relating to God—Study Guide (BWP001088)	$2.35	_____	_____
Genesis: People Relating to God—Large Print Study Guide (BWP001089)	$2.75	_____	_____
Genesis: People Relating to God—Teaching Guide (BWP001090)	$2.95	_____	_____
Genesis 12—50: Family Matters—Study Guide (BWP000034)	$1.95	_____	_____
Genesis 12—50: Family Matters—Teaching Guide (BWP000035)	$2.45	_____	_____
Leviticus, Numbers, Deuteronomy—Study Guide (BWP000053)	$2.35	_____	_____
Leviticus, Numbers, Deuteronomy—Large Print Study Guide (BWP000052)	$2.35	_____	_____
Leviticus, Numbers, Deuteronomy—Teaching Guide (BWP000054)	$2.95	_____	_____
1 and 2 Samuel—Study Guide (BWP000002)	$2.35	_____	_____
1 and 2 Samuel—Large Print Study Guide (BWP000001)	$2.35	_____	_____
1 and 2 Samuel—Teaching Guide (BWP000003)	$2.95	_____	_____
1 and 2 Kings: Leaders and Followers—Study Guide (BWP001025)	$2.95	_____	_____
1 and 2 Kings: Leaders and Followers Large Print Study Guide (BWP001026)	$3.15	_____	_____
1 and 2 Kings: Leaders and Followers Teaching Guide (BWP001027)	$3.45	_____	_____
Ezra, Haggai, Zechariah, Nehemiah, Malachi—Study Guide (BWP001071)	$3.25	_____	_____
Ezra, Haggai, Zechariah, Nehemiah, Malachi—Large Print Study Guide (BWP001072)	$3.55	_____	_____
Ezra, Haggai, Zechariah, Nehemiah, Malachi—Teaching Guide (BWP001073)	$3.75	_____	_____
Job, Ecclesiastes, Habakkuk, Lamentations—Study Guide (BWP001016)	$2.75	_____	_____
Job, Ecclesiastes, Habakkuk, Lamentations—Large Print Study Guide (BWP001017)	$2.85	_____	_____
Job, Ecclesiastes, Habakkuk, Lamentations—Teaching Guide (BWP001018)	$3.25	_____	_____
Psalms and Proverbs—Study Guide (BWP001000)	$2.75	_____	_____
Psalms and Proverbs—Teaching Guide (BWP001002)	$3.25	_____	_____
Matthew: Hope in the Resurrected Christ—Study Guide (BWP001066)	$3.25	_____	_____
Matthew: Hope in the Resurrected Christ—Large Print Study Guide (BWP001067)	$3.55	_____	_____
Matthew: Hope in the Resurrected Christ—Teaching Guide (BWP001068)	$3.75	_____	_____
Mark: Jesus' Works and Words—Study Guide (BWP001022)	$2.95	_____	_____
Mark: Jesus' Works and Words—Large Print Study Guide (BWP001023)	$3.15	_____	_____
Mark:Jesus' Works and Words—Teaching Guide (BWP001024)	$3.45	_____	_____
Jesus in the Gospel of Mark—Study Guide (BWP000066)	$1.95	_____	_____
Jesus in the Gospel of Mark—Teaching Guide (BWP000067)	$2.45	_____	_____
Luke: Journeying to the Cross—Study Guide (BWP000057)	$2.35	_____	_____
Luke: Journeying to the Cross—Large Print Study Guide (BWP000056)	$2.35	_____	_____
Luke: Journeying to the Cross—Teaching Guide (BWP000058)	$2.95	_____	_____
The Gospel of John: Light Overcoming Darkness, Part One—Study Guide (BWP001104)	$3.55	_____	_____
The Gospel of John: Light Overcoming Darkness, Part One—Large Print Study Guide (BWP001105)	$3.95	_____	_____
The Gospel of John: Light Overcoming Darkness, Part One—Teaching Guide (BWP001106)	$4.50	_____	_____
The Gospel of John: Light Overcoming Darkness, Part Two—Study Guide (BWP001109)	$3.55	_____	_____
The Gospel of John: Light Overcoming Darkness, Part Two—Large Print Study Guide (BWP001110)	$3.95	_____	_____
The Gospel of John: Light Overcoming Darkness, Part Two—Teaching Guide (BWP001111)	$4.50	_____	_____
The Gospel of John: The Word Became Flesh—Study Guide (BWP001008)	$2.75	_____	_____
The Gospel of John: The Word Became Flesh—Large Print Study Guide (BWP001009)	$2.85	_____	_____
The Gospel of John: The Word Became Flesh—Teaching Guide (BWP001010)	$3.25	_____	_____
Acts: Toward Being a Missional Church—Study Guide (BWP001013)	$2.75	_____	_____
Acts: Toward Being a Missional Church—Large Print Study Guide (BWP001014)	$2.85	_____	_____
Acts: Toward Being a Missional Church—Teaching Guide (BWP001015)	$3.25	_____	_____

Item	Price		
Romans: What God Is Up To—Study Guide (BWP001019)	$2.95	_____	_____
Romans: What God Is Up To—Large Print Study Guide (BWP001020)	$3.15	_____	_____
Romans: What God Is Up To—Teaching Guide (BWP001021)	$3.45	_____	_____
Galatians and 1&2 Thessalonians—Study Guide (BWP001080)	$3.55	_____	_____
Galatians and 1&2 Thessalonians—Large Print Study Guide (BWP001081)	$3.95	_____	_____
Galatians and 1&2 Thessalonians—Teaching Guide (BWP001082)	$3.95	_____	_____
Ephesians, Philippians, Colossians—Study Guide (BWP001060)	$3.25	_____	_____
Ephesians, Philippians, Colossians—Teaching Guide (BWP001062)	$3.75	_____	_____
1, 2 Timothy, Titus, Philemon—Study Guide (BWP000092)	$2.75	_____	_____
1, 2 Timothy, Titus, Philemon—Teaching Guide (BWP000093)	$3.25	_____	_____
Letters of James and John—Study Guide (BWP001101)	$3.55	_____	_____
Letters of James and John—Large Print Study Guide (BWP001102)	$3.95	_____	_____
Letters of James and John—Teaching Guide (BWP001103)	$4.25	_____	_____
Revelation—Study Guide (BWP000084)	$2.35	_____	_____
Revelation—Large Print Study Guide (BWP000083)	$2.35	_____	_____
Revelation—Teaching Guide (BWP000085)	$2.95	_____	_____

Coming for use beginning December 2011

Item	Price	
The Gospel of Matthew: A Primer for Discipleship—Study Guide (BWP001127)	$3.95	_____
The Gospel of Matthew: A Primer for Discipleship—Large Print Study Guide (BWP001128)	$4.25	_____
The Gospel of Matthew: A Primer for Discipleship—Teaching Guide (BWP001129)	$4.95	_____

Standard (UPS/Mail) Shipping Charges*			
Order Value	Shipping charge**	Order Value	Shipping charge**
$.01—$9.99	$6.50	$160.00—$199.99	$24.00
$10.00—$19.99	$8.50	$200.00—$249.99	$28.00
$20.00—$39.99	$9.50	$250.00—$299.99	$30.00
$40.00—$59.99	$10.50	$300.00—$349.99	$34.00
$60.00—$79.99	$11.50	$350.00—$399.99	$42.00
$80.00—$99.99	$12.50	$400.00—$499.99	$50.00
$100.00—$129.99	$15.00	$500.00—$599.99	$60.00
$130.00—$159.99	$20.00	$600.00—$799.99	$72.00**

Cost
of items (Order value)   _____

Shipping charges
(see chart*)   _____

TOTAL   _____

*Plus, applicable taxes for individuals and other taxable entities (not churches) within Texas will be added. Please call 1-866-249-1799 if the exact amount is needed prior to ordering.

**For order values $800.00 and above, please call 1-866-249-1799 or check www.baptistwaypress.org

Please allow three weeks for standard delivery. For express shipping service: Call 1-866-249-1799 for information on additional charges.

YOUR NAME _____ PHONE _____

YOUR CHURCH _____ DATE ORDERED _____

SHIPPING ADDRESS _____

CITY _____ STATE _____ ZIP CODE _____

E-MAIL _____

MAIL this form with your check for the total amount to
BAPTISTWAY PRESS, Baptist General Convention of Texas,
333 North Washington, Dallas, TX 75246-1798
(Make checks to "Baptist Executive Board.")

OR, **FAX** your order anytime to: 214-828-5376, and we will bill you.

OR, **CALL** your order toll-free: 1-866-249-1799
(M-Fri 8:30 a.m.-5:00 p.m. central time), and we will bill you.

OR, **E-MAIL** your order to our internet e-mail address:
baptistway@texasbaptists.org, and we will bill you.

OR, **ORDER ONLINE** at www.baptistwaypress.org.

We look forward to receiving your order! Thank you!